The Gambian Cookbook

Recipes from The Smiling Coast

(c) 2011

Michele Daryanani
Shakhil Shah

Michele Daryanani and Shakhil Shah have asserted their right to be identified as the authors of this work in accordance with the Copyright, Designs and Patents Act 1988. Special thanks to Elena Sikdar for support while compiling the manuscript.

Published by :
The Saharan Press, part of the Eo Vita Group.
20 Blossom Way, Hillingdon, Middlesex, UB10 9LN
United Kingdom
The Saharan Press is the imprint division of the Eo Vita group.

ISBN : 978-1-908797-00-1

Catalogue copies of this publication are available from:
- o The British Library
- o Bodleian Library, Oxford
- o Cambridge University Library
- o National Library of Scotland, Edinburgh
- o The Library of Trinity College, Dublin
- o National Library of Wales, Aberystwyth

Summary: A cookbook collection of typical recipes and authors' favourites from The Gambia, West Africa.
File Under: Cookbooks

This publication is printed on recyclable paper.

Dedicated to the women in our lives,

who always push us to pursue our dreams.

Table of Contents

Introduction

The Gambia - or more often known as the smile in the West African Coast, is a small country enclaved in Senegal. Over the centuries, political, religious and personal interests have caused cultures to step on The Gambia's sunny banks, and along with them, a diverse palate of sensory delights. Chief amongst these, the food, who's history bears influences from around the world - yet each with its subtle modifications to make it Gambian.

We, the authors, spent most of our lives in Gambia - and certainly all of our formative years. Going to an international school in The Gambia meant that we were exposed to both sides of the table - the fiery Gambian dishes as well as the "toubab" dishes imported from around the world, which are gradually being adapted and incorporated into the dishes that will be served as traditional Gambian in the years to come.

Over the course of this recipe book, we hope to make you discover an array of Gambian recipes, ranging from the most elementary plain white rice, to the more complex dishes like Cherreh.

It is said that cooking Gambian food is an art-form. If that is the case, then serving Gambian food is the canvas - and this needs to be set up properly! The key ingredient is family and friends. You cannot eat alone, that is the first and foremost rule. If you are alone, and have cooked Gambian food, invite your neighbour, the lady walking her dog, your colleague and the corner-shop clerk. The more, the merrier!

Next on the list is the dish. Traditionally, Gambian food is served, and eaten, out of a single common bowl using your hands as utensils. This can be served on the floor or on a table. For the average non-Gambian, this can be a little intimidating - so while you should still serve the food out of a common bowl, make sure each guest has their own plate, fork, spook and knife. The plate should be plain white - this will contrast well again the tablecloth, which should be brightly coloured. Ideally, try to use a tie-dye tablecloth.

If you cannot find a tie-dye table-cloth, make your own. It takes a few minutes more than washing a tablecloth, and the results are unique. To do this, take a white cotton tablecloth (80% or greater cotton), a few elastic bands and a packet of washing machine dye. Lay the tablecloth flat, then pinch the middle of the tablecloth and pull upwards. Place an elastic band about 2 centimetres from the top (where you pinched it), wrapping it around enough to make it very tight. Repeat the process, with an elastic band every 3-5 centimetres, until the entire tablecloth is wrapped into a think long cylinder, similar to a pony-tail. Make sure that all the elastic bands are very tight, then put into a washing machine following the instructions on the dye pack. This will make a tie-dye tablecloth with concentric rings, perfect for your meal!

As decoration, put some fresh, bright tropical flowers in the middle of the table. These will brighten up the atmosphere and give a focal point before you bring the food. If your guests will be eating after dark, make sure you have candles as well - you never know when G.U.C. (now NAWEC) will cut the light! (and they do make a great romantic atmosphere)

Finally, drinks. Make sure there is an ample supply of cold water along with ice-cold, glass-bottled, Coca-Cola or some of the drinks from the drinks section of this book.
The only thing left to say is "Na si jamm-barre!"

Special Ingredients & Terms

The following ingredients are typical to Gambian cooking. Where possible (and necessary) suitable substitutes are presented.

Aubergine

Aubergines, originally came from India. Commonly known also as eggplant and garden eggs, the variety used in The Gambia tends to be smaller and a bit more bitter than their Eastern counterparts. These should be available in your normal grocery store.

Bananas

Bananas normally do not need to be described however there are a few important facts about Gambian bananas that should be noted, first of all they are not as yellow as the bananas purchased in Europe or the United States. The Gambian banana is greenish yellow in colour and usually covered in brown spots. Another important distinction is that these bananas tend to be smaller and much sweeter than the ones bought in Europe or the United states. When exporting bananas, producers will pluck them green from the trees and ship them in containers filled with gas. This causes them to ripen in the store and not on the tree. Sadly, along with the shelf life, the taste is also affected.

Baobab

The baobab fruit is the fruit found inside the pods that grow on baobab trees. The pods are ripe when they are a green to brown colour. All one needs to do is break open the pod and take out the fruit inside. The baobab fruit is almost like a creamy white pulp that covers the seeds inside the pod. The pulp ranges; a soft moist pulp to quite dry and almost chalk like in texture. The fruit can be used in a variety of ways, eaten as is, used in drinks, porridges and a few other ways.

Beans

Beans are a staple world-wide. For any Gambian

recipes that require beans, any dry bean will work (from kidney beans to black eye beans). If using fresh beans, try to use French string beans or mange-tout.

Bitter Tomato (Jaxato)

The Bitter tomato is a fruit found in Africa, it is pale green to yellow in colour and used in soups, stews and in a lot of savour dishes. The bitter tomato is also used as a thickener in soups and stews, and has the interesting antiseptic capacity, which helps dishes last longer. In theory if you do not cannot find bitter tomatoes, Tamarilo may work as a substitute.

Casava

Cassava, which is also known as manioc, is a plant which has an edible root which is used in West African cooking in much the same way as potatoes are used in Western cooking. The cassava root and leaves

are also used in West Africa. You can find cassava in most grocery stores, fresh and sometimes frozen. Interestingly, while growing, cassava stores cyanide in its roots - which is then eaten!

Coconut

Coconuts are another fruit found in abundance in West Africa, coconuts have many applications, and the meat of the coconut is used in many dishes as is the water.

Coriander

Coriander actually comes from the orient, but has become a staple to add flavour to dishes world-wide. It has an intense pungent flavour, and in Gambia is usually grown by the collective farms.

Ginger

Another seasoning from the orient, ginger was imported to Egypt by the Roman conquerors who found that it would transport well over long voyages.

Gren-Gren

Gren-Gren (also known as "krain krain", "West African Sorrel" and "Bush Okra" in The Gambia) is a green leaf of the Corchorus family and is used in a multitude of Gambian dishes. Once cooked, it has a slightly slimy texture (similar to Okra). The taste is similar to sorrel leaves once cooked.

If you cannot find Corchorus olitorius (Jute Leaf) in your local grocery shop, substitute this with an equivalent portion of spinach, sorrel or sweet potato leaves mixed with a few finely chopped okra pods and the juice of a lime.

Kani

Kani (Kaani, Kanni) is the Wolof name for chilli in The Gambia - which usually refers to local chilli peppers (a type of scotch bonnet). It is an extremely hot/spicy chilli but is the essence of most, if not all, Gambian dishes. If you cannot get Gambian scotch bonnet you could substitute it with normal scotch bonnet chillies or habernero peppers but this will change the flavour of the dish. An alternative is to use "Aggy's Hot Chilli & Spices Sauce" (http://www.aggyssauces.com/) - the flavour is as close to a traditional Gambian kani as I've tried!

Maggi

Maggi and Jumbo are the most popular bouillon cubes used in West African cooking. Both are easy to find in your local grocery shops. It must be said that you should use the cubes and not the sauce as there is a difference in taste. Both the terms Maggi and Jumbo are copyright of their respective companies and have no association with this book.

Mango

Mangoes are a fruit that originated in India and has since spread throughout the world. In the Gambia mango is used in much the same way as in any other country in the world, it is eaten as a fruit or used in cooking. Mangoes are a seasonal fruit, there are many different varieties of mangoes, and each variety has its own distinctive flavour as well as size and colour. Mangoes are available in most grocery stores; however for the best mangoes one should always go to a specialist Asian or African grocery store.

Millet

Millet is a grain that has been used in West African cooking for quite some time. Millet is believed to originate in Ethiopia, but like most things they were brought over centuries ago and have become a staple in West African cooking as well. Used both in sweet and savoury cooking, millet is readily available at most African/Asian grocery stores.

Okra

Okra also known as Lady Fingers, are another vegetable found in the Gambia. Okra is a vegetable that is found in many cultures and cuisines, know by different names. In The Gambia, it is used in soups and stews. Available in your local grocery stores this can also be found in the frozen food section in some stores. As a preference one should always use fresh as opposed to frozen. If you want to avoid it's slimy effect, quickly pan fry it with a little salt before cooking.

Palm Oil

Palm oil is derived from the Oil Palm is dark red almost

orange in colour and has quite a distinctive flavour. It is widely available in African markets or grocery stores as pure un-refined palm oil (which looks like a solid wax - this will melt when heated). Try to avoid blends (e.g. palm oil mixed with canola oil).

Parsley

Parsley is a herb that is renown globally - interestingly, it was through to have been spread by the Vikings!

Peanuts

Peanuts, or groundnuts, are a very important crop in Gambia. Used both as a source or edible oil and protein, it is one of the few crops that are grown on a commercial scale throughout The Gambia. The typical groundnut used in Gambian cooking is the Bambara Groundnut, which can be eaten fresh, boiled or roasted (amongst other ways). This has a very high protein content (up to 18%), which makes it an ideal substitute for more expensive, animal-based, proteins. Using any other peanut or groundnut (unsalted and unroasted!) will work for most recipes in this book.

Plantain

Plantains are from the same family as bananas but differ from bananas in that they are not as sweet, larger and unless completely ripe cannot be eaten raw. They ripen in much the same way to bananas in that they start green, then go to yellow, and at their ripest become black. Plantains can be used at any stage of ripeness and can be prepared in a multitude of ways; boiled, steamed, grilled, fried and roasted. You can find them in grocery stores situated in African and Afro-Caribbean neighbourhoods.

Rice

Rice is considered one of the key staples around the world. Believed to originate in the Niger delta, the domestication of rice as a crop has led to its production in swampy areas. Sadly, most of the rice consumed in The Gambia is imported or donated from other countries. To achieve a truly Gambian flavour, use "broken rice" as a pose to "whole grain" basmati. Avoid Japanese (sticky) and Italian (risotto) rice.

Sipa-Sipa

Sipa-sipa is the Wolof word for shrimps or prawns. They both work well in most recipes, but skewering small shrimps may prove challenging! Raw prawns/shrimps are grey with white flesh. If buying pre-cooked prawns, these will already be pinky-orange with white flesh. If buying frozen prawns, do not defrost these in water as they will lose flavour. Instead, put them in a bowl in the fridge overnight.

Sweet Pepper

Sweet pepper is one of the 3 key ingredients in The Gambian flavour (the other two being kani and tomato). In some parts of the world they are known as bell peppers or capsicum.

Tapalapa

Tapalapa is the West African equivalent to the traditional French Baguette. Although it looks like the French baguette, Tapalapa is not a light; in fact it will keep you going until lunch or dinner time. Traditionally, it is baked in a wood-fired, mud-oven.

Yam

Yams are a root vegetable similar to Cassava and should not be mistaken with what the Americans or Canadians refer to as yams.

The American/Canadian
Yam is more commonly
known as Sweet potato.
Yams are extremely
versatile, in The Gambia
they are used in much the
same way to Cassava,
boiled, fried or pounded
into Fufu. Yam flour can
also be used to make cakes.
They are not too difficult to
find, they are easily found in
Asian and African grocery
stores as well as Afro
Caribbean stores.

Yate

Yate is Wolof for the triton -
a very large, ocean dwelling
snail. Reaching sizes in
excess of 40-50 centimetres
while living by scavenging
the ocean's floor - these
snails are the garbage
collectors of the ocean.
Sometimes found in
African/Caribbean stores,
they can be replaced with
large quantities of abalone,
oysters, mussels or clams.

Snacks

Snacks and nibbles play an important role in
Gambian nutrition. Be it a simple cassava chip, or
a more complex fish cake - they are equally good
at staving off hunger!

Akra Dipping Sauce

A spicy sauce ideal for use with Akras or as a sauce to spice up chips/fries, it even goes well with Afra lamb

15-20 Minutes   Simple

Ingredients:

- 1 can of tomato concentrate paste (50g)
- 1 onion sliced finely
- 2 cloves of garlic chopped or minced
- 2 to 3 kani chillies finely chopped
- juice of 1 to 2 Lemons
- 1 teaspoon of black pepper corns
- 2 tablespoons of peanut oil
- 1 teaspoon of salt
- ½ cup of water

Method:

1. In a heavy pan heat up the oil and add the black pepper and sliced onions until they start to brown, (about 2 minutes), then add the chopped garlic and cook for an additional minute.
2. Add the can of tomato puree to the pan and continue to cook until the oil begins to separate from the tomato mixture, at this point add the chopped kani chillies and 1 cup of water.
3. Once the water comes to a boil turn the heat down and simmer until the sauce reduces by half. Add the salt and lemon juice. The sauce is now ready.

While "designed" for Akra fritters, this sauce is spectacular with just about any savoury Gambian dish!

To make an even more spectacular chilli sauce, just double the quantity of kani chillies. The resulting sauce can be used to spice up any dish.

Akra Fritters

A bean fritter that originated in West Africa, it is crispy on the outside with a soft smooth centre. There are several variations and the name may differ from one region to another. Akra and its variations are also popular in Brazil, Haiti and several other countries outside of Africa, where slaves were sent from Western Africa.

30 Minutes   Simple

Ingredients:

- 500g of black-eyed peas, soaked in water over night
- 1 large onion
- 1 kani chilli
- 5-6 black pepper corns
- Salt to taste

Method:

1. After the beans have soaked in water overnight, drain in a colander and place back in the bowl, cover with water and rub the beans until the skins come off and float to the surface. Discard the skins and drain.
2. Place the beans, onion, black pepper corns and ½ the kani in a blender and blitz until you have a thick paste, you may have to add a little water to the mixture so that is blends properly. Add salt to taste, you can add the other ½ of the kani if you want it to be a bit spicier.
3. In a pan add enough oil to have about 5 centimetres of oil in the pan or alternatively use a deep fryer. Using a

teaspoon, drop a spoonful of the batter into the hot oil and cook until golden brown on all sides. Take out of oil and place on kitchen towel or newspaper to drain the oil.

4. Once all are made, serve with the Akra dipping sauce, recipe provided in the book.

As a short cut you could use canned black-eyed peas, however as a personal preference I would not as the texture of the blended mixture is not quite the same.

There are a few variations to the recipe above, should you not wish to use the onions you can omit it from the recipe. Alternatively you can sauté the onion until golden brown and add that to the bean paste.

Another alternative would be the use of dried shrimps, you can either add ½ a cup of dried shrimp to the beans prior to blending, or you can place a single dried shrimp in to the middle of the bean paste prior to frying for a surprise filling.

Cassava & Plantain Chips

A great snack made from cassava and plantain to be eaten anytime. These chips are extremely popular in many parts of Africa and are a personal favourite. Goes down well with beer, particularly an ice cold Julbrew!

The cassava and the plantain should be prepared individually. You will also need a mandolin slicer.

30 Minutes   Simple

Ingredients:

- 1 kilograms of Cassava
- 1 kilograms of Plantain
- Salt & Chilli powder to taste
- Enough oil to fry with.

Method:

For the Cassava Chips;
1. Peel the cassava and place in a bowl of cold water (this must be done to stop the cassava from going black).
2. Heat the oil up in a large pot/pan.
3. Once scalding take the cassava out and slice directly into the oil.
4. Fry for about 2 minutes or until golden brown remove and place on old newspaper to let the oil drain.
5. Repeat the process until all the cassava is done.

6. Once cooled sprinkle with salt you can add the chilli powder should you wish.

For the Plantain Chips;
1. Heat the oil up in a large pot/pan until scalding hot
2. Once hot peel the plantain and slice the plantain directly into the oil.
3. Fry for about 2 minutes or until golden brown remove and place on old newspaper to let the oil drain.
4. Repeat the process until all the plantain is done.
5. Once cooled sprinkle with salt you can add the chilli powder should you wish.

In addition to the salt and chilli powder you can squeeze lemon juice on top of the chips. Note that this should only be done before serving, if left for too long the chips will become soggy.

Do not peel the plantain too early or it too will go black!

Cassava Fries

A great alternative to potato fries, and a staple at any gathering with friends.

30-40 Minutes   Simple

Ingredients:

- 500grams of cassava
- 1 cup peanut oil
- Juice from 2 lemons
- Salt & Chilli powder to taste

Method:

1. Boil the cassava until cooked, once cooked allow to cool.
2. Cut into approximately 2 inch long by ½ inch wide pieces.
3. Heat up some oil in a pan or alternatively in a deep fryer.
4. Cook the cassava until golden brown and crisp.
5. Drain on paper towels.
6. Just before serving sprinkle with salt, chilli powder and lemon juice

Replace the chilli powder with black pepper for a milder taste.

Chawarma

Chawarma is another recipe that has been "imported" to the Gambia. With the recipe's origin in Lebanon, "Shawarmas" were brought to the Gambian table by the myriad of Lebanese take-away restaurants.

Probably the most famous amongst these was Ali Baba in Banjul - note, this wasn't Ali Baba the restaurant but a tiny Chawarma joint next to the market in Banjul. Of equal fame (to me at least) was the Chawarma joint on Pipeline road (now renamed to Kairaba avenue). The place changed names every few months, but in my memory it will always be Atsons' Chawarma (due to the fact it was next to the original Atsons supermarket before it relocated). Reminiscing aside, the recipe below is my favourite; and I can't help but feeling hungry typing this!

3 Hours   Moderate

Ingredients:

- 1kilograms tender goat, beef or lamb fillet meat
- 4 large pita breads
- 2 large potatoes
- 4 tablespoons oil
- 1 medium onion, finely chopped
- 2 kani chillies, finely chopped
- 2 tomatoes, finely chopped
- 2 teaspoons coriander, finely chopped

Marinade:

- ¼ cup lemon juice
- ¼ cup vinegar

- ¼ cup peanut oil
- 1 tablespoon mustard
- 1 teaspoon salt

Sauce:
- 4 tablespoons hummus
- 2 teaspoons tahini
- 2 tablespoons plain yogurt
- 2 tablespoons lime juice

Method:

1. Mix all the ingredients for the marinade together.
2. Put the meat and marinade in a ziplock bag, and leave in a fridge overnight.
3. In a hot skillet or non-stick pan, cook the meat until medium rare.
4. Remove the pan from the heat, and slice the meat into very thin slips.
5. Slice the potatoes into strips and fry in the oil.
6. Split the pita in half so you have 8 thin disks.
7. For each Chawarma, put two disks on top of each other, overlapping by a few centimetres.
8. Put the fries, meat, onion, kani, tomatoes and coriander in the pita.
9. Add the 4 "sauces" (hummus, tahini, yoghurt, lime juice) to the pita and roll up.
10. Enjoy immediately!

Adjust the quantities of the 4 sauces to taste, personally, I love more yoghurt and less tahini!

Dibbi

Dibbi is one of the first sights tourists see as they arrive in The Gambia. As the bus takes them from the airport, on the roadside (especially the old road that went through Serrekunda) they would see street-sellers making Dibbi. Dibbi is the Gambian version of the kebab.

25 Minutes   Simple

Ingredients:

- ∾ 500 grams beef, cubes
- ∾ 5 onions, cut into chunks
- ∾ 2 tablespoons vinegar
- ∾ 1 tablespoon black pepper
- ∾ 1 teaspoon kani, finely chopped
- ∾ 1 clove garlic, finely chopped
- ∾ 1 tomato, finely chopped
- ∾ 2 tablespoons peanut oil
- ∾ Wooden skewers

Method:

1. Mix all the ingredients except the onions in a large bowl, ensuring the meat is thoroughly covered.
2. Marinate overnight.
3. Put the meat and onions on the skewers, alternating them.
4. Grill on a wood or coal fire until the meat is well done.
5. Serve with bread, sprinkled with Maggi.

Egg & Mayo Sandwich

While it may seem odd that this recipe is not in the toubab section, this is truly a Gambian tradition. Go to any Mauritanian corner shop, and ask for an egg sandwich and this is what you'll get. The following recipe makes 4 sandwiches.

5 Minutes   Simple

Ingredients:

- ❧ 2 Tapalapa baguettes
- ❧ 4 eggs, hardboiled and peeled
- ❧ 4 tablespoons mayonnaise
- ❧ 2 large Maggi cubes

Method:

1. Cut the Tapalapa lengthwise.
2. Coat the inside of the bread with the mayonnaise.
3. Cut the egg into disks, and lay in the bread.
4. Crumble the Maggi and spread over the egg.
5. Serve immediately!

There are two important differences from the Western Egg & Mayo Sarnie. The first is the bread, which is crusty. The second is the use of the Maggi, which adds complexity to an otherwise bland recipe.

Fish Cakes

These fishcakes were "exported" to the Caribbean with the slave trade, and live there to this day. While very sad, the fact that this recipe has survived on both sides of the Atlantic is a testament to its simplicity and flavour.

15 Minutes   Simple

Ingredients:

- 500 grams cooked fish
- 500 grams boiled cassava, mashed
- 2 eggs, beaten
- 100 grams breadcrumbs
- 1 kani chilli, finely chopped
- 1 small Maggi cube
- ½ teaspoon ground black pepper
- Oil for frying

Method:

1. Flake the fish into small pieces, then gently mix it with the cassava mash.
2. Add the eggs, kani chilli, crushed Maggi cube, and black pepper to the mash - mix well.
3. Heat the oil in a pan until scalding.
4. Roll the fish into balls about 5 centimetres wide, then gently flatten. This forms a flatter, wide oval.
5. Dip the oval in breadcrumbs and fry until golden brown.
6. Serve warm with chilli sauce, ketchup or Akra sauce.

Karang Sandwich

A homebrew favourite which I still dream of. Every time I bite into this sandwich I get teleported back to Karang. When we would drive to Dakar, we would first pass the Gambian border, then would need to wait several hours while the Senegalese formalities were sorted. Ideally enjoyed in a car with no a/c in the sweltering heat. The ideal way to use this time was to prepare the Karang Sandwich (the name was coined from the village where we ate it) and the recipe is my father's version.

10 Minutes   Simple

Ingredients:

- 2 Tapalapa baguettes
- 2 cans of sardines in oil
- 1 kani chilli
- 1 large onion
- 2 large Maggi cubes

Method:

1. Drain the sardines and put into a bowl.
2. Finely dice the kani and onion and add to the sardines.
3. Mix thoroughly, breaking up the sardines.
4. Cut the Tapalapa lengthwise and spread the sardine paste inside.
5. Crush the Maggi cube and sprinkle liberally over the paste.
6. Cut each baguette in half, making 4 sandwiches.

Meat Pies

Sitting in my father's shop during the afternoons I would wait with anticipation the arrival of the pie seller. A young chap, carrying a large cloth covered bowl. Underneath would be the best pies you could get on the planet. Small morsels of heaven, they came in two flavours - meat or spinach. (Note that the spinach was not vegetarian as there was some meat juice sprinkled in for flavour!) .The recipe below gets pretty close to those meat pies.

15 Minutes   Complex

Ingredients:

- 300 grams beef mince
- 200 grams Gambian Pouched Rat mince (or turkey/pork)
- 1 tablespoon peanut oil
- 1 large onion, finely chopped
- ½ tin of canned tomatoes, drained and finely diced
- 2 tablespoons peas
- 2 tablespoons potatoes, cut into small cubes
- 2 large Maggi cube
- ½ teaspoon curry powder
- ½ teaspoon black pepper
- ½ teaspoon salt
- 6 cups flour
- 200 grams margarine, room temperature
- 1 teaspoon baking soda
- 1 cup water
- 5 eggs, beaten

Method:

1. Heat the oil in a deep non-stick pan.
2. Stir fry the meat, Maggi, half the onion, the peas, the potatoes and the spices on high heat until the juices have dried up.
3. Add the rest of the onion and the tomatoes and 1 Maggi cube.
4. Simmer on low heat for 15 minutes, or until the juice from the tomatoes mix has dried up.
5. Set aside and allow to cool.
6. Preheat oven to 200C.
7. In the meantime, prepare the pastry dough.
8. In a large bowl, thoroughly mix the flour, baking powder and margarine (this should look like granules).
9. Add 4 beaten eggs (keep 1 aside for the glaze) and mix well.
10. Add the water, 1 tablespoon at a time, and knead.
11. Repeat step 10 until an elastic dough is obtained.
12. Split the dough into 12 equal balls, lightly dust these with flour to prevent them from sticking.
13. With a rolling pin, flatten the balls into oval shaped, about half-a-centimetre thick.
14. Add 2 tablespoons of meat mixture to one side of the dough.
15. With a brush, put some of the remaining egg onto the edge of the dough, then fold the dough over to form a semi-circle shaped pie.
16. Dust a fork with flour, then press down on the curved edge of the pie to seal it.

17. Place on a baking sheet and brush the top with some of the egg (to make a shiny glaze).
18. Bake for 40 minutes (or until golden brown).
19. Allow to cool before attempting to remove from the baking tray.

My mother generally doesn't like meat - that said, these pies were one of those things she loves! Try dipping these in the Akra Sauce and you'll see why!

Peanut Butter

While commonly called peanut butter in Gambia, a little known fact is that in reality there are multiple types on peanuts. The type grown in Gambia is the Bambara Groundnut, and difficult to find other than in Western Africa. That said, the common peanut will work just as well for this recipe, which is adapted from the lady on Bakau market who would make it and sell it alongside her peanuts.

10 Minutes   Simple

Ingredients:

- 500 grams Bambara groundnuts (or peanuts)
- ½ teaspoon salt
- ½ teaspoon sugar
- 1 tablespoon peanut oil (optional)
- 1 kilograms of sand

Method:

1. Put the sand in a large pan on medium heat.
2. Add the peanuts - roast the peanuts until the pop and their skins darken; then allow to cool.
3. Remove the sand from the peanuts with a sieve.
4. Remove the skin from the peanuts by pressing between your fingers.
5. Put the peanuts in a meat mincer and grind. Mix the oil, salt and sugar in with the peanut paste.
6. Re-grind through the mincer, repeatedly, until the peanut butter is smooth.

Spinach Pies

An almost vegetarian alternative to the meat pies, Gren-Gren pies are another import from the middle east to Gambia.

15 Minutes   Simple

Ingredients:

- 6 cups flour
- 200 grams margarine, room temperature
- 1 teaspoon baking soda
- 1 cup water
- 1 Maggi cube
- 2 tablespoons beef drippings (optional)
- 250 grams Gren-Gren leaves, finely chopped
- 1 small onion, finely chopped
- 3 tablespoons lime juice
- 2 teaspoons peanut oil
- ½ teaspoon salt
- ¼ teaspoon pepper

Method:

1. In a bowl, mix the flour, salt, and margarine - then knead thoroughly.
2. Gradually add water, 1 tablespoon at a time, kneading constantly, until the dough is elastic.
3. Split dough into balls 5 centimetres in diameter and set aside.
4. Preheat oven to 200°C.
5. Mix all the other ingredients together to create the filling.

6. With a rolling pin, flatten the balls into a round shaped disk.
7. Add 1 tablespoons of filling mixture to the centre of the disk.
8. Fold the dough in from three sides, to form a triangle shaped pastry.
9. Bake for 40 minutes (or until golden brown).
10. Allow to cool before attempting to remove from the baking tray.

The meat drippings are optional. Traditionally, some minced meat would be sprinkled into the Gren-Gren filling "to add flavour" - but replacing this with a stock cube of taking it out altogether will work just as well.

Sweet Fire Peanuts

In Bakau market there was a little old lady who always had a peanut for me as a kid. Whenever I would go there alone, she would ask about my mother, and when my mother would go she would ask about me. The following recipe is based on the peanuts she would sell, little bites with a sweet-and-spicy coating, perfect as a snack while haggling in the market!

90 Minutes   Moderate

Ingredients:

- 1 cup water
- 2 cups sugar
- 4 cups of peanuts
- 2 tablespoons hot chilli powder

Method:

1. Preheat oven to 150°C.
2. Mix the water and sugar in a non-stick frying pan over high heat.
3. At the sugar melts into a syrup, lower the heat to a medium heat and add the peanuts.
4. Stir regularly, until the peanuts are evenly coated and there is no syrup left in the pan.
5. Add the chilli powder, and spread the peanuts on a baking tray.
6. Bake in the over until the sugar syrup is dry, this may take 30-60 minutes.
7. Let the peanuts cool before enjoying them!

Tapalapa

Tapalapa is a traditional bread, similar to an artisanal baguette. Very filling in nature, I would sneak to the local Mauritanian boutique (corner shop) on weekends and get a Tapalapa filled with eggs, mayo and Maggi.

While traditionally cooked in a wood-burning, mud oven, a suitable replacement can be made in a gas or electric oven. For extra authenticity, sprinkle with a little dust at the end of cooking ! The bread will store for a few days, and then can be converted into bread pudding or used in bullet.

3 Hours   Moderate

Ingredients:

- 800grams Wheat Flour
- 100g Corn flour
- 50grams Millet flour
- 1 teaspoon dry baking yeast
- 1 teaspoon baking powder
- 600milliliters Cold water
- 10grams ice cubes
- 2 teaspoons salt
- 1 cup of water
- 1 tablespoon of sugar

Method:

1. Mix the wheat flour, corn flour, millet flour, yeast, and baking powder in a large bowl.
2. Dissolve the salt in the 600milliliters of water, then add the ice cubes.
3. Gradually add the cold, saline solution to the flour, kneading constantly.
4. Knead until a uniform, elastic dough is obtained.
5. Cover the dough with a clean linen or cotton cloth, and leave to rest in a dark place for 1 hour.
6. Separate the dough into equal pieces of approximately 250grams each.
7. Roll the pieces into rods, about 25cm in length.
8. Cover with a clean linen or cotton cloth and allow to rest in a dark place for 1 hour.
9. Preheat the oven to 200°C.
10. With a sharp knife, draw 3 diagonal lines on each baguette.
11. Dissolve the sugar in a cup of water.
12. Paint each baguette with the sugary water - this helps give the crust it's golden colour.
13. Bake for 35 minutes, or until the crust is a deep golden brown.
14. Remove the Tapalapa baguettes from the oven and allow to cool on a wire rack.

Tapalapa makes an amazing accompaniment to any stew, on its own or as sandwich bread.

Mains

Gambian cooking poses an interesting challenge for the recipe author. Dishes cannot be divided into the traditional fish, poultry and meat categories as most dishes use a mixtures of protein sources. Similarly, most dishes eaten in Gambia can be
eaten for lunch or dinner - thus negating the use of that division system. Either way, the dishes for a main part of the meal - hence, they all fall within this chapter in alphabetical order.

Afra

A traditional street food of grilled lamb and onions.

30 Minutes   Simple

Ingredients:

- 0.5kilogramss Lamb cubed into .05 to 1 inch cubes
- 2 large onions sliced
- 2 magi cubes
- 1 kani chillies (you can add more if you like)
- 1 teaspoon black pepper
- 2 cloves garlic
- 5 tablespoons of oil

Method:

1. Put the lamb in a large bowl and with the sliced onions, kani chillies (chopped) and the magi cubes (crumbled).
2. This is a dish that is cooked outside on a wood fire or coal fire. Traditionally, this is cooked on a grill with a small mesh - that said, you can place the lamb on skewers alternating the lamb with the sliced onion. Rub with oil and place on the grill until cooked (10 to 15 minutes).
3. If the weather isn't great you can cook the lamb in a cast iron skillet, heat the oil in the skillet once hot add the lamb and onions and cook on a high heat for about 10 minutes or until the lamb is cooked. To make the process

easier, cook the lamb in batches with the sliced onion, this will give you more control the cooking of the lamb.

As an alternative to the above recipe you can make a marinade for the lamb to add a bit more flavour. What I normally do is: Blend 1 medium onion, the garlic, black pepper to taste and the magi cubes until a smooth paste is formed. Rub that all over the lamb and set aside for a minimum of 1 hour or for best results overnight.

Once the lamb is marinated follow the process for the traditional Afra above. Omitting the magi cubes as they have already been added to the marinade.

Bassi Nyebbeh

This is a traditional Gambian dish made with beans which are then served with palm oil based gravy.

1 Hour   Moderate

Ingredients:

- 500g of Black eyed beans, soaked overnight
- 2 large onions sliced
- 300milliliters palm oil
- 1 kani (you can add more if you like)
- Salt & Pepper to taste
- 2 tablespoons of tomato puree

Method:

1. Once the beans have soaked, remove the skin by rubbing the beans with your hands, the skins should float to the top of the water which will make it easy for you to remove.
2. After you have skinned the beans, drain them and place in a saucepan with water, cook until the beans are tender about 1 hour (you can reduce cooking time by placing in a pressure cooker).
3. Whilst the beans are cooking you can prepare the gravy, in a saucepan or frying pan heat up the palm oil, add the onions and cook until they soften, add the tomato puree and kani, cook for a few more minutes. At this point add

1 to 2 cups of water and continue to cook until the gravy thickens slightly.

4. When the beans are done, drain and crush/mash slightly.

Server the bean mash with the gravy on top, steaming hot.

Beef & Oil Stew

The name gives away the recipe - a simple stew that (for once) does not include any chilli pepper! (though you certainly can add some if you want that kick).

2.5 Hours   Moderate

Ingredients:

- 500 grams of stewing beef with bones, cut into cubes
- ½ cup of palm oil
- 2 tablespoons tomato concentrate paste
- 750 millilitres water
- 100 grams of pumpkin flesh, cut in cubes
- 100 grams of Gren-Gren or spinach
- 1 sweet peppers, seeds removed and chopped
- 2 cloves of garlic, crushed
- 2 onions, peeled and chopped
- 2 tomatoes
- ½ cup vinegar
- 1 large Maggi cube
- 1 tablespoon black pepper, ground
- Salt & pepper to taste

Method:

1. Marinade the beef in the vinegar, garlic and black pepper for 4 hours (overnight preferably).
2. Heat the palm oil, then fry the meat in it until golden brown. Ensure you keep the vinegar sauce!
3. Add the chopped onions, and fry until soft.

4. Add the rest of the ingredients and simmer for 2 hours. During this time, the pumpkin will go soft once it is cooked, remove it at this point or it will disintegrate.
5. After the 2 hours, the meat should be tender and fall off the bone. Re-add the pumpkin, and serve hot, over rice.

While this recipe specifies beef, this can be done with mutton or lamb and it'll be equally delicious!

Beef Benachin

Benachin quite literally means "one pot" (bena is one in Wolof, and chin is pot). This is because to cook this most iconic of dishes, you need only one large pot. That means, that if you are using more than one pot to cook this, you are cheating!

2 Hours   Moderate

Ingredients:

- 1kilogram of beef or mutton, cut into large cubes
- 500milliliters of peanut oil
- 4 tablespoons tomato concentrate paste
- 100 grams tomatoes, finely diced
- 1 large onion, chopped
- 2 bay leaves
- 1 litre of water
- 500grams of rice
- 1 teaspoon cayenne pepper
- 2 large Maggi cubes
- 200 grams of carrots, cut in half
- 200 grams of pumpkin, cut in 4 pieces
- 200 grams of aubergine (eggplant), cut into 4
- ½ cabbage, cut into 4
- 3 kani chillies
- Salt & pepper to taste

Method:

1. In a deep pan, heat the oil until scalding.

2. Deep fry the meat until cooked throughout, then remove and set aside.
3. Add the chopped onions, tomatoes, tomato puree and cayenne to the hot oil.
4. Stir for 2 minutes on medium heat.
5. Add water, 2 Maggi cubes, 2 kani chillies, bay leaves and the vegetables.
6. Simmer for 30 minutes.
7. As the vegetables cook, remove and keep warm (the aubergine should cook first and the carrot last).
8. Add the rice to the pan (still containing the simmering juices) and stir well.
9. Bring to the boil, then reduce heat and simmer for 15-30 minutes (until the rice has soaked up all the water and is tender and cooked).
10. Serve the rice with the vegetables and meat on top.

Traditionally, benachin is made with beef, mutton, chicken and/or fish - potentially all together if you can afford all of them. I have split the recipes into fish, chicken and beef/mutton; I did this to showcase three very different ways to cook the benachin. The actual meat used is just a particular!

Beef Stew

Very similar to the beef & oil stew, this version is a little healthier as it doesn't include as much oil! It also is spicier, and less green.

2.5 Hours   Moderate

Ingredients:

- ✎ 500 grams of stewing beef with bones, cut into cubes
- ✎ 1 tablespoon peanut oil
- ✎ 3 potatoes, peeled and cut into cubes
- ✎ 2 slices of cabbage
- ✎ 2 tablespoons tomato concentrate paste
- ✎ 750 millilitres water
- ✎ 1 sweet peppers, seeds removed and chopped
- ✎ 2 cloves of garlic, crushed
- ✎ 2 onions, peeled and chopped
- ✎ 2 tomatoes
- ✎ 1 kani chilli, finely chopped
- ✎ ½ cup vinegar
- ✎ 1 large Maggi cube
- ✎ 1 tablespoon black pepper, ground
- ✎ Salt & pepper to taste

Method:

1. Marinade the beef in the vinegar, garlic and black pepper for 4 hours (overnight preferably).
2. Heat the peanut oil, then fry the meat in it until golden brown. Ensure you keep the vinegar sauce!

3. Add the chopped onions, and fry until soft.
4. Add the rest of the ingredients and simmer for 2 hours. During this time, the potato and cabbage will go soft once it is cooked, remove them at this point or they will disintegrate.
5. After the 2 hours, the meat should be tender and fall off the bone. Re-add the potatoes and cabbage, and serve hot - over rice.

Putting everything in a pressure cooker and cooking for 30 minutes also works quite well!

Bonga with Okra

I spent many Sundays on the back of a pickup truck on the way back from Brufut picking and eating at the load of Bonga my father had just bought. The strong smell, very similar to lapsang souchong tea , is special and the smoked Bonga from Brufut is sold all over The Gambia. Bonga is a type of shad fish (Ethmalosa fimbriata) that is commonly smoked for transport and storage.

The following is a simple dish with huge potential to please the palate. Not only is the flavour unique, but the texture that the stewed okra give it is very unique. Once cooked, the stew should have an almost slimy texture.

60 Minutes   Moderate

Ingredients:

- 4 smoked and dried Bonga
- 500milliliters water
- 12 okra
- 1 onion sliced into strips
- 4 tablespoons palm oil
- 3 tbsp tomato concentrate paste
- 1 kani pepper
- salt and black pepper

Method:

1. Preheat oven to 180°C.
2. Remove the head, tail and skin from the fish and discard.
3. Separate the flesh from the bones and discard the bones.

4. Put the fish and water in a oven bowl and add Salt & Pepper.
5. Bake for 30 minutes at 180°C.
6. Remove the tips of the okra, then slice into thin rings.
7. Heat palm oil in a deep frying pan and brown the onion slices until golden.
8. Add the tomato paste, then stir for 2 minutes on medium heat.
9. Remove from the heat, then stir in the okra rings and add to the fish.
10. Put everything in the oven and bake for 20 minutes, stirring occasionally.
11. Serve over Fufu or plain white rice.

If you cannot find Bonga, replace with a smoked fish

Bullet

Bullet, or fish balls is one of the most classical Gambian dishes. There are as many variations to the bullet recipe as there are types of fish in Gambian waters (if not more). The following recipe is a combination of various methods, which, over the years has become my favourite.

1 Hour   Moderate

Ingredients:

- 500grams fresh white-fish (barramundi, cod, sea bass, hake, perch, tilapia all work well)
- 2 large kani peppers
- 150milliliters of water
- 4 large onions
- 1 bay leaf
- 2 Large Maggi cubes
- 50 grams of baguette type bread
- ½ cup of milk (optional)
- 4 tablespoons millet flower
- half a bunch of finely chopped parsley
- 1 teaspoon of hot chilli powder
- 2 teaspoons of lemon juice
- 1 egg (optional)
- 3 tablespoons of Palm oil
- 3 tablespoons of corn or vegetable oil
- 3 cloves of garlic
- 3 tablespoons of tomato concentrate
- 2 cups of tomatoes

Method:

1. Skin, gut and bone the fish; then dice into small pieces.
2. Finely dice& chop 2 of the onions, 1 clove of garlic, 1 kani pepper, and the parsley then mix in a large mortar & pestle with the fish.
3. Soak the bread in the milk (optional) or in half a cup of water then add to the mortar & pestle.
4. Add 1 teaspoon of salt to the mix, 1 Maggi cube, the millet flour and optionally add 1 egg to the mix; then pound until the paste is homogeneous.
5. Oil your hands, and form the paste into small balls, about 1-inch in diameter.
6. Heat the palm oil and corn/vegetable oil in a frying pan, then add the fish balls a few at a time.
7. Stir and fry until the balls are browned on all sides - then set aside.
8. Repeat until all the fish balls are cooked. Keep the oil!
9. Finely chop the remaining onions, garlic cloves and tomatoes .
10. Add the chopped onions and garlic to the hot oil, stir until the onions are golden.
11. Add the remaining ingredients to the onions (chopped tomatoes, remaining (whole) kani pepper, bay leaf, Maggi cube, hot chilli powder, lemon juice, tomato concentrate and 150milliliters water) and bring to a boil.
12. Simmer for 15 minutes, stirring constantly.
13. Add the cooked fish balls to the stew, then simmer for a further 5 minutes.

14. Add salt and black pepper to taste.
15. Serve over plain white rice.

In absence of a mortar & pestle, use a food blender!

Bullet also works great with spaghetti as an alternative to meatballs!

Casamance Stew (Caldo)

A traditional one pot stew of fish onions and chilli, which is eaten in the southern part of Gambia and in Casamance, or Southern Senegal.

2 Hours   Moderate

Ingredients:

- 1cup fresh lemon juice OR lime juice (you can use ½ a cup of white vinegar and ½ a cup of lemon/lime juice as an alternative)
- 4 tablespoons peanut oil (2 for the marinade and 2 for cooking)
- 1 teaspoon fresh ground black pepper
- 2 magi cubes dissolved in 2 tablespoons of warm water and left to cool
- 3 cloves of garlic minced
- 2 Kani or more to make it spicier
- 1 -2 catfish
- 4 medium onion sliced
- 1 sweet potatoes, cut in 1-inch cubes
- 2-3 carrots cut in 1-inch cubes
- 1 red bell pepper chopped (optional)
- salt, to taste

Method:

1. In a glass bowl combine the juice of lemon/lime, peanut oil, black pepper, magi cubes, garlic, kani , and the onions. This will become the marinade for the fish.

2. Cut the fish into large chunks , rinse and add to the marinade. Leave the fish in the marinade for a minimum of 2 hours, for best results overnight.
3. Once the fish is marinated, remove the fish and spate the onions from the remaining liquid. Keep the liquid for use in the sauce.
4. Place the sweet potatoes and the carrots in a pot with cold water with some salt, bring to the boil and cook until just tender, remove from heat and place in cold water to stop it from cooking any more. Drain and place aside.
5. Whilst the vegetables are cooking, heat up the remaining oil in a heavy bottomed pan and sauté the onions from the marinade, cook until golden brown about 15 minutes, you can add the bell peppers at this stage if you are using them. Now add the vegetables and the leftover marinade sauce to the onions and simmer for 15 to 20 minutes.
6. Whilst the vegetables are simmering in the sauce, brown the fish on all sides in a skillet or for best results on a grill. Once browned add to the vegetables and cook for a further 15 minutes or until the fish is cooked through.
7. Serve on rice.

As an alternative to the fish you could use chicken however this would be deemed to be more of a Yassa than Casamance Stew. I also like to add a few more vegetables such as aubergine (egg plant) which can be added to the onions when cooking.

Casava Leaf Stew

Cassava stew is a variation of the classic Soupa Kanja. A little less slimy in texture, and much thicker, this tends to appeal to younger palates more than the classic Soupa Kanja.

1.5 Hours   Moderate

Ingredients:

- 500 grams of cassava leaves
- 1 cup of black-eye or kidney beans
- 1 cup of peanut paste or peanut-butter
- 2 smoked Bonga fish
- 1 smoked medium cat fish
- 500 grams goat meat, cubed
- 1 sweet pepper
- 8 tomatoes
- 3 shallots
- 2 onions
- 300 grams of locust beans (carob beans)
- 1 cup of palm oil
- 1 Maggi cube
- 1 kani chilli
- 1 litre of water
- Salt & pepper to taste

Method:

1. Bring 1 litre of water to the boil then add the goat.
2. Mince the cassava leaves until finely chopped, then add to the boiling water.
3. Debone the Bonga and catfish, then add to the boiling water.
4. Pound the locust beans, sweet pepper, kani, onions, shallots, and tomatoes in a mortar & pestle (or blend in a blender).
5. Add the peanut paste and Maggi cube, stir well then cover.
6. Simmer until the water dries up (about 40 minutes).
7. All the palm oil, then simmer for a further 20 minutes.
8. Serve with boiled white rice!

If you cannot find fresh carob beans, replace with locust bean gum

Catfish Stew

One of the many variations of fish-based dishes, the following catfish stew recipe contains no green leaves. Very popular around Brufut, I used to see women cooking this while waiting for their husbands to return with nets full of fish!

1.5 Hours   Moderate

Ingredients:

- 800 grams smoked catfish
- 1 litre water
- 2 large onions, chopped
- 5 tablespoons tomato concentrate paste
- 3 bay leaves
- 3 kani chillies
- 500milliliters peanut oil
- 2 tablespoons palm oil
- 3 gloves garlic, crushed
- 2 carrots, cut into disks
- 2 large Maggi cubes
- 1 large tomato, chopped
- 1 medium cassava, cut into 2-inch cubes
- 1 small cabbage, cut into 8
- Juice from 1 lime
- Salt & Pepper to taste

Method:

1. Remove the flesh from the catfish's bones, discard bones.
2. In a large pan, heat the oils until scalding.
3. Blend the onions, tomatoes, tomato paste, garlic and one of the kani chillies.
4. Deep dry the tomato mix in the oil, stirring constantly.
5. Add 1 litre of water and Maggi cubes and bring to a boil.
6. When boiling, add all the other ingredients except the lime juice.
7. Reduce heat and simmer for 45 minutes.
8. Serve with white rice and sprinkle with lime juice.

Adjust the Maggi cubes to taste - they replace salt in this recipe!

Cherreh

Cherreh is one of the most labour intensive dishes in the Gambian repertoire - to make it properly this takes 7 days to prepare! The recipe below assumes you have winnowed (husked) millet and as such takes a lot less time.

3 Days   Complex

Ingredients:

> For the Cherreh:
- 1 kilograms of Millet (if using millet flour skip to step 5)
- Water

> For the sauce:
- 500 grams Baobab leaves, finely chopped
- 200 grams dried fish
- 2 okras, sliced into disks
- 500 grams beef, cubed
- 250 grams of peanuts, crushed
- 2 small Maggi © cubes
- 2 large onions fine
- 2 litres water
- 2 large green or red peppers, sliced
- 2 kani chillies
- Salt & Pepper to taste

Method:

1. Pound the millet with a mortar & pestle, or process in a food blender until all the millet is broken up.

2. Put the millet in a large bowl and gradually add water until all the millet is moist.
3. Allow to dry overnight, then sieve.
4. Repeat steps 1-3 until the all millet reaches the consistency of fine flour.
5. Gradually add cold water to the millet while kneading - keep adding water until a springy dough is formed.
6. Allow the dough to rest overnight - the fermentation process will give the Cherreh a sour taste.
7. Form balls about 5 centimetres in diameter from the Cherreh dough.
8. Steam for 30 minutes - the Cherreh will become firm and change colour from white to light brown.
9. Boil the baobab leaves and okra in 2 litres of water.
10. Strain the leaves and okra, set the water aside.
11. Add all the other ingredients except for the sweet peppers to the water and bring to a boil.
12. Simmer for 2 hours, or until the beef falls apart when prodded.
13. Add the spinach and okra mix, as well as the peppers.
14. Simmer for a further 10-15 minutes, or until the peppers are cooked.
15. To serve, place a few warm Cherreh balls on a plate, then cover with the baobab sauce.

As with most recipes, there are endless variations of this. If you cannot find baobab leaves, this can be done with spinach, Gren-Gren or other green leaves.

Chicken Benachin

Traditionally, benachin is made with chicken and beef (and/or fish) - this recipe uses only chicken, and as such, is great when catering for people who don't eat beef. Additionally, this adds another variation to the benachin method.

2 Hours   Moderate

Ingredients:

- 1 medium chicken
- 5 cloves of garlic, peeled & finely chopped
- 3 tablespoons vinegar
- ½ cabbage, cut into 4 pieces
- 2 bitter tomatoes
- 5 tomatoes, chopped
- 1 large aubergine, cut into 4-8 chunks
- 200grams of pumpkin without seeds/skin, cut into 4 chunks
- 3 onions, finely chopped
- 1 cup peanut oil
- 1 cup palm oil
- 3 tablespoons tomato concentrate paste
- 1 sweet pepper, seeds removed and finely chopped
- 3 kani chillies
- 2 large Maggi cubes
- 4 cups rice
- 2 bay leaves
- Salt & Pepper to taste

Method:

1. Wash the chicken and cut into portion-sized pieces; e.g. legs, thighs, wings, breast, etc.
2. Pat dry the chicken.
3. Mix the vinegar, garlic, 1 teaspoon salt and 1 teaspoon pepper in a blender.
4. Coat the chicken with the seasoning paste and allow to marinate in a refrigerator for a few hours.
5. Heat the 2 oils in a large pan.
6. When hot, add the chicken, and fry until thoroughly cooked (approximately 5-10 minutes).
7. Remove the chicken from the pan, and add the onions, fry until golden brown.
8. Add all the vegetables (tomatoes, sweet pepper, bitter tomatoes, aubergine, pumpkin, cabbage) and cook for 10-15 minutes - as the vegetables go soft and are cooked, remove from the pan.
9. Add all the other ingredients to the pan, and cover with 6 cups of water.
10. Bring to a boil on high heat and boil for 5 minutes, stirring constantly.
11. Lower the heat and simmer until all the water is absorbed and the rice is cooked (20 minutes approximately).
12. Serve the vegetables and chicken on a bed of the rice.

Chicken Yassa

Chicken Yassa is undoubtedly one of my favourite dishes. So much so that after we moved away from The Gambia, I taught the cook at my new school how to cook it. After making it just once, the demand from the other students and teachers was so great that he made is a regular dish! This dish is also great on a hot Sunday BBQ - just marinade it the night before!

2 Hours   Moderate

Ingredients:

- 1 chicken, cut into pieces (or 4 chicken thighs and 4 chicken legs)
- 3 kani chillies, finely diced
- 6 large onions, cut into strips
- 4 large Maggi cubes
- 3 tablespoons yellow mustard
- 10 cloves of garlic, peeled
- 1 cup of vinegar
- Juice from 4 limes
- 2 tablespoons peanut oil
- Salt & Pepper to taste

Method:

1. In a large bowl, prepare the marinade by mixing all the ingredients together bar the oil. Crush the Maggi before adding it to aid in mixing.
2. Allow the mix to sit in the fridge, thus marinating the chicken, overnight.

3. When ready to cook, heat the oil in a large, non-stick pan.
4. Once scalding hot, fry the chicken, one piece at a time until golden brown on the outside. Set aside the chicken.
5. Once all the chicken is golden brown, add the marinate and juices to the pan as well as the chicken.
6. Stirring constantly, simmer for 45 minutes. The chicken should be cooked throughout, and the onions soft and yellow.
7. Serve with white rice.

If preparing for a BBQ, cook the marinade in a pan and the chicken on the BBQ. This will ensure that you still have the great sauce to go with it!

Choo

Choo, or chew, is a beef stew with a kick. Considered a "rich" dish due to its content of expensive meat, it can be made with the off-cuts of beef stewed until tender. A pressure cooker is a modern addition that makes a once time consuming dish quick and easy!

1.5 Hours   Moderate

Ingredients:

- 500 grams beef, diced
- 1 litre of water
- 2 cups of peanut oil
- 4 onions, diced
- 4 large tomatoes, diced
- 50 milliliters of tomato concentrate paste
- 2 cloves of garlic
- 2-3 kani chillies
- ½ a cabbage, cut into 4 pieces
- 8 small aubergines (max 5 centimetres in diameter)
- 500 grams of cassava, chopped into large cubes
- 1 sweet pepper, quartered
- 4 carrots, peeled and halved

Method:

1. Pound the onions, tomatoes, garlic, and kani chillies in a mortar & pestle (or blender) - leave aside 1 whole kani chilli.
2. Heat the oil in a pressure cooker until scalding hot.

3. Add the meat and allow to deep fry until cooked.
4. Mix the tomato paste, spice mix and the litre of water, then add to the pressure cooker.
5. Seal and bring to pressure.
6. Allow to cook under pressure for 20 minutes.
7. Remove from the heat, allow to cool enough to open the pressure cooker.
8. Add the remaining ingredients and simmer for a further 10-15 minutes, until the vegetables are cooked and the gravy has thickened.
9. Serve over warm white rice.

The beef should fall apart when prodded once the dish is cooked - slightly fattier beef will work well as the fat will melt into the stew and flavour the dish.

Domoda

Domoda is a traditional stew that needs very little introduction. When growing up, Saturdays were Domoda days. Every Saturday at lunchtime the entire family would congregate, along with a few friends, forming a dozen strong group of people all eager to relish the Domoda!

1-2 Hours   Moderate

Ingredients:

- 2 cups Homemade peanut butter (see recipe) alternatively you could use any store bought crunchy peanut butter
- 1 – 2 kani chillies
- 700g stewing beef cubed into 1 inch cubes
- 1 -2 large onions chopped
- 1 can chopped tomato
- 1 table spoon tomato puree
- 2 cloves garlic
- ½ White Cabbage cut into 6 pieces
- 1 butternut squash cubed into 1 to 2 inch cubes
- 4 Jaxato (if available)
- 1 – 2 lemons or limes juiced
- ¼ cup oil
- 2 magi cubes
- Water to cover

Method:

1. In a large heavy bottomed pot, heat the oil and brown the meat and onions. Once browned, add the tomato puree and cook for about 3 minutes. Now add the vegetables and seasonings (kani, magi, garlic) and cover with water.
2. Once the water comes to the boil, reduce the heat, take a ladle of the water and work into the peanut butter until you have a watered down paste, add this mixture to the pot and bring back to the boil then reduce the heat and continue to simmer for 45 – 60 minutes.
3. Keep stirring the sauce and if it starts to get too thick add a little more water. You may find that the oil from the peanut butter will float to the top, this can be removed if you wish.
4. Serve with rice.

An alternative way of cooking would be to cook the vegetables separately in boiling water, you can also add 2-3 carrots and aubergine. Once cooked keep on the side and serve on the side with the meat.

You can also substitute the beef with chicken should you wish or alternatively completely omit the meat and make a vegetarian version.

Ebbeh

Ebbeh is a dish that is believed to originate in Nigeria. That said, over the centuries, the Gambian version has been modified and adapted to become a unique red pot of flavour and spice. Great on those colder evenings sitting by a bonfire on the beach!

2 Hours   Simple

Ingredients:

- 1kilograms of cassava, peeled and cut into pieces
- 200 grams smoked Bonga fish, deboned
- 200 grams smoked catfish, deboned
- 200 grams prawns, shell removed
- 100 grams crab claws or flesh, shell removed
- 100 grams oysters, shells removed
- 2 cups palm oil
- 3 kani chillies
- 20g black tamarind pulp
- 2 large Maggi cubes
- Juice from 3 limes

Method:

1. In a large pan, bring 2 litres of water to a boil.
2. Add the cassava, and boil until the cassava is soft. When prodded with a fork, it should go in easily.
3. With a potato masher, mash the cassava in the pot.
4. Add the remaining ingredients and simmer for 20-30 minutes, or until a deep red chowder is obtained.
5. Serve piping hot!

New Town Stew

New Town or Brikama Stew was a favourite of a friend of ours who has a very colourful past. Having worked in South Africa, Sierra Leon, and just about every area with conflict - he wasn't the typical Gambia who would blend in a crowd. In fact, at over 2 meters, blonde hair and blue eyes he really quite stuck out of a crowd! The recipe below was first savoured while sitting on a house made of shipping containers stacked on top of each other, overlooking Casamance while discussing the finer points of tear gas. Ensure you have enough kani chillies to make this recipe!

2 Hours   Moderate

Ingredients:

- 3 pig's feet, thoroughly washed
- 500grams of smoked catfish (or other smoked fish)
- 1 litre of water
- 5 onions
- 5 tomatoes
- ½ a cabbage, cut into 4
- 1 medium cassava, peeled and cut into 8 pieces
- 3 kani chillies, 1 of which should be finely chopped
- 1 sweet pepper, finely chopped
- 3 limes, juiced
- 3 bay leaves
- 3 tablespoons of tomato concentrate paste
- 1 large Maggi cube
- 3 cloves of fresh garlic, peeled and finely chopped
- 300milliliters of peanut or palm oil (or a blend of the two)
- Salt & Pepper to taste

Method:

1. Put the smoked fish in a large bowl, cover with the water and then add the lime juice.
2. Allow the fish to soak for 15 minutes
3. Cut the pig's feet in half, and wash again. Remove any hair if there is any by quickly burning the hair off over a gas stove.
4. Heat the oil in a deep pan, then add the pigs feet and stir fry until the skin is golden.
5. Add all the remaining ingredients bar the fish (which is still soaking), the cabbage and the cassava. Then, fry on high heat for 10-15 minutes - stirring constantly to avoid burning. If the mix goes dry, add some water from the bowl where the fish is soaking.
6. Add the fish and the water it's been soaking in to the pan, stir well.
7. Simmer for 2 hours, or until the flesh on the pigs feet is falling off the bone.
8. Add the cabbage and cassava, then simmer for a further 30 minutes (or until the cassava is cooked).
9. Serve over white rice or crusty bread.

My parent's love a variation of this recipe, without the smoked fish and with allspice added. Give it a try! The pigs feet release a sticky gelatine which gives the whole stew a sticky feel to it - dipping some bread in works great!

Fish Benachin

"Grandpa" was our P.E. teacher, Mr. Cham. Why we called him grandpa, I can't explain; but he made a mean fish benachin. Being one of the most popular (if not THE most popular) Gambian dish, there are thousands of variations. The recipe below is adapted from Grandpa's original!

2 Hours   Moderate

Ingredients:

- 400 grams fresh firm fish (sea bass, snapper or tilapia work well)
- 3 cups of rice
- 1 cup of peanut oil
- ½ cup of palm oil
- 2 large onions
- 8 fresh tomatoes
- 4 tablespoons of tomato paste concentrate
- 200 grams of salt fish (dry salted fish)
- 2 slices of yateh (water snail)
- 6 kani chillies
- 4 cloves garlic
- 2 large Maggi cubes
- 2 tablespoons of parsley, finely chopped
- 2 teaspoons black peppercorns
- salt & black pepper
- ½ cabbage
- 4 carrots
- 4 small potatoes

- 4 okra
- 4 bitter tomatoes
- 2 aubergines
- 1 slice of pumpkin
- 1 sweet pepper

Method:

1. Clean the fresh fish, removing the skin, guts, bones, head and tail. Coat with salt.
2. Cut the salt fish and yateh into 2-3 inch chunks.
3. In a mortal & pestle, pound the black peppercorns, Maggi, sweet pepper, garlic, onion and 4 of the kani chillies.
4. In a large pan, heat the peanut and palm oils until very hot.
5. Deep fry the fish, salt fish, and yateh (one piece at a time) until all sides are golden brown and the fish is cooked throughout.
6. Drain and set the fish aside on a paper napkin to absorb the oil.
7. In the same pan, keep the oil hot and ass the pounded ingredients and tomato paste. Stir well and simmer for 2 minutes.
8. Add 1 cup of water and bring to a boil.
9. Peel the remaining vegetables and cut into large chunks - add to the pan.
10. Add 4 cups of water and bring to a boil.
11. Once the vegetables are cooked, remove from the broth and set aside.

12. Measure the broth - add enough water to make 8 cups of broth.
13. Add the rice, and bring to a boil.
14. Reduce the flame to a low heat and keep stirring until all the water is absorbed and the rice is cooked.
15. To serve, lay the rice in a bowl and put the vegetables and fish on top.

If you cannot find Yate, you can replace this with shelled mussels or clams.

Fish Stew

This fish stew always reminded me on the old-Denton bridge (a.k.a. Oyster Creek Bridge) while Piggy (my dog) ate a pile of rancid, dry shrimp heads abandoned there by fishermen over the years. No idea why, but it's I reckon it's because this soup is what we made with our fish!

45 Minutes   Simple

Ingredients:

- 500 grams of fish fillets (red snapper is ideal), uncooked
- 5 okras, chopped
- 100 grams of pumpkin
- 2 tomatoes, chopped
- 1 sweet pepper, seeds removed and chopped
- 1 aubergine, chopped into cubes
- 100milliliters of palm oil
- 3 onions, chopped
- 4 tablespoons of lime juice
- 1 tablespoon of tomato concentrate puree
- 1 teaspoon of yellow mustard
- 1 pint of water
- Salt & Pepper to taste

Method:

1. Marinade the fish fillets with the lime juice for 30 minutes.
2. Heat the oil, then fry the fish until golden on both sides. Remove the fish from the pan.

3. Fry the onions until soft, then add all the other ingredients to the pan.
4. Simmer for 20 minutes - then add the fish and stir. This will cause the fish to flake and mix with the vegetables.
5. Simmer the lot for a further 5-10 minutes, then serve hot!

As with most Gambian dishes, adding a kani chilli makes this dish pop to life!

Fufu

Fufu is an African staple used as an alternative to rice. There are different types of Fufu, it can be made with any of the following: Cassava, Yams, Plantain or Coco-yams. The traditional method is quite time consuming and labour-intensive. However there is an easier way to prepare Fufu, which you will find in the closing comments.

1 Hours   Moderate

Ingredients:

- 1kilograms Cassava
- Salt to taste (about 1 teaspoon)
- Water

Method:

1. Peel the cassava and place in a pot of water bring to the boil and cook until the cassava is soft and tender (approximately 40 minutes).
2. Drain the cassava and place into a large pestle and mortar. Pound the cassava until it becomes a soft and smooth consistency. Add salt to taste and you are done.
3. Serve warm with any Gambian soup as a sauce.

The cassava can be substituted with Plantains, coco-yams, yams or even potato. The process is exactly the same irrelevant of which staple you choose. As an alternative you can purchase pre ground cassava or plantain flour mix with boiling water to make Fufu (although this is cheating!).

Mbahal

Mbahal is one of those dishes that every Gambian knows, but no two people will have the same recipe. The following recipe is for a rich and filling recipe, with enough energy to satisfy anyone for the entire day.

2 Hours   Moderate

Ingredients:

- 500grams of white fish
- 200grams of dry, salted fish
- 100grams of smoked, dry Bonga fish (optional)
- 2 cups of rice, washed
- 2 limes, juiced
- 100grams of locust beans or black-eye beans
- 2 tomatoes, chopped
- 2 onions, chopped
- 1 bunch of spring onions
- 200milliliters of peanut or palm oil
- 1 cup of peanuts, crushed
- 100grams of pumpkin, cleaned and cubed
- 2 small aubergines, cut into large cubes
- 3 bitter tomatoes, cut in half
- 2 large Maggi cubes
- 3 kani chillies
- ½ a cabbage head, cut in four
- 2 sweet peppers, seeds removed
- Salt & Pepper to taste

Method:

1. Clean the fresh fish and wash the dry fish in clean water (scrape/scrub this to remove the excess salt).
2. Cut the fish in portion-sized pieces and coat with salt, black pepper and lime juice.
3. In a mortar & pestle, pound the beans, sweet peppers, and tomatoes until a paste is obtained.
4. Heat the oil in a large, deep pan.
5. Fry the onions until soft and golden brown.
6. Add the fish and deep fry for 2 minutes.
7. Add the pounded paste, then fry for 2 minutes.
8. Add the pumpkin, aubergine, cabbage, Maggi and bitter tomatoes to the pot.
9. Add 4 cups of water, and all the other ingredients to the pot except the rice.
10. Bring to a boil, then simmer for 15 minutes (or until the vegetables are cooked).
11. Remove the vegetable chunks and fish from the stock and set aside.
12. Add the rice and simmer for 20 minutes (or until the rice is cooked and the water absorbed).
13. To serve, create a bed of rice and serve the fish and vegetables over the top.

Some like to add extra sauce to this; a tamarind, tomato and garlic being a favourite.

Mbahal Sauce

A perfect sauce to complement the Mbahal, this rich blend of tamarind, tomatoes and garlic will wake up any dish!

15 Minutes   Simple

Ingredients:

- 50 grams of locust beans, blended (or locust bean powder)
- 50 grams of sour tamarind pulp
- 7 cloves of garlic, peeled
- 3 onions, finely chopped
- 1 sweet pepper, seeds removed
- 3 tomatoes
- 2 teaspoons tomato concentrate paste
- ½ cup peanut oil
- 2 kani chillies (more to taste)
- 1 teaspoon black pepper, finely ground
- 1 Maggi cube

Method:

1. Heat the oil and fry the onions until golden brown.
2. Mix all the remaining ingredients in a blender - blend until smooth.
3. Add the paste to the hot oil and simmer for 5 minutes, stirring constantly.
4. Serve warm.

Nyebbeh with Oil Gravy

Every weekend I would sit at the Jimpex corner where my father had a shop and watch the world go by. On the other side of the road was a stall selling food throughout the day. In the morning, amongst other things, they had Nyebbeh - a bean mash typically served for breakfast with an oil based gravy. A truly tasty treat, which with a little Tapalapa can go a long way.

90 Minutes   Simple

Ingredients:

For the Nyebbeh:

- 600g dry kidney or black-eye beans
- salt

For the Oil Gravy:

- 300 millilitres of palm oil
- 50 milliliters of groundnut oil
- 2 onions
- 2 tablespoons of tomato concentrate
- 300milliliters water
- Salt and Black pepper to taste

Method:

1. Soak the beans overnight in water with a pinch of salt to soften the skin.
2. Remove the skins from the beans - to do this, rub the now soft skin which should peel off.

3. Cover the beans with salted water and add a pinch of salt.
4. Bring to a boil on high heat, then reduce the heat and simmer for 60 minutes (until the beans are tender).
5. Drain the beans and mash to a consistency similar to mashed potatoes then set aside.
6. In a separate pan, heat the oils to prepare the gravy
7. Once the oil is hot, add the onion (finely diced) and tomato concentrate.
8. Once the onions are golden brown, add 300milliliters of water and a pinch of salt.
9. Simmer until most of the water has evaporated and the sauce attains the consistency of gravy.
10. Serve the mashed beans (Nyebbeh) with the gravy poured on top.

Okra Stew

Okra is a unique ingredient. Depending on how it is cooked, it can turn an entire dishes consistency into a slimy stew. If stir-fried a little first with salt, the slimy effect is avoided - this simple stew on the other hand, makes full use of the sliminess. This is a slight variation of the traditional supa-kanja, and becomes a lot more slimy.

2 hours   Moderate

Ingredients:

- 200 grams stewing beef, cubed
- 500 grams fresh okra, washed
- 2 sweet peppers, seeds removed
- 1 smoked Bonga (or other smoked fish)
- 1 bitter tomato, whole
- 1 large onion, finely diced
- ½ cup palm oil
- 1 teaspoon black pepper
- 1 kani, finely chopped
- 1 tablespoon castor oil
- Salt & Pepper to taste

Method:

1. Wash the smoked fish, and debone.
2. Cut the okra into small disks.
3. Dice the sweet pepper flesh.
4. Heat the palm oil in a large pot, and fry the beef until brown on the outside.

5. Add all the remaining ingredients bar salt, and 2 litres of water.
6. Bring to a boil, then reduce the heat and simmer for 30 minutes.
7. Remove the bitter tomato, then simmer for a further hour, until the stew is gooey.
8. Add salt to taste, and re-add the bitter tomato before serving.

Make sure you don't add the salt until the end - the lack of salt allows the okra's sliminess to fully develop.

Oyster Stew

Similar to an oyster chowder, the mighty mangroves along the Gambia river have influenced this dish and transformed it into a rich, spicy delicacy!

2 Hours   Moderate

Ingredients:

- 200 grams of oysters
- 2 tablespoons of palm oil
- 2 tablespoons of lime juice
- 2 tablespoons of black pepper
- 3 onions, chopped
- 3 cloves of garlic, crushed
- 3 tomatoes, chopped
- 3 tablespoons of tomato concentrate paste
- 1 kani chilli, finely chopped
- 500 millilitres of water
- 1 bay leaf
- 1 sweet pepper, seeds removed
- 100 grams of pumpkin flesh
- Salt & Pepper to taste

Method:

1. Heat the palm oil, then fry the onions, garlic and oysters until the onions are soft.
2. Remove the oysters from the oil, then add all the other ingredients.

3. Bring to a boil, and simmer for 30 minutes stirring constantly.
4. All the ingredients should disintegrate into a pulp, to speed this up, a potato masher can be used.
5. Re-add the oysters, and simmer for a further 10 minutes.
6. Serve hot, with some crusty bread on the side!

If using a pressure cooker, leave a quarter of the oysters in the pressure cooker to give the stew more flavour - then add the rest before serving!

Pepe Soup - Chicken

The traditional chicken pepe soup is known as a cure-all; in fact, it's been called the Gambian chicken soup. Beware though - it packs quite a punch!

3 Hours   Moderate

Ingredients:

- 250 grams of tomato concentrate paste
- 500 grams of chicken, cut in small pieces
- 2 litres of water
- 1 tablespoon of black pepper, finely ground
- 2 tablespoons of kani chilli, finely chopped
- 2 whole kani chillies
- 1 teaspoon of salt
- 1 clove of garlic, crushed
- 2 large Maggi cubes
- 2 tablespoons of peanut oil

Method:

1. Mix the black pepper, chopped kani, garlic, and Maggi in a blender and blend until smooth.
2. Heat the oil in a deep pan.
3. Stir fry the chicken until cooked, then add the paste from the blender and the water.
4. Bring to a boil.
5. Simmer until the stock has halved.
6. Add the tomato paste and stir until it has been incorporated into the stock.

7. Simmer for 10 further minutes.

8. Serve steaming hot, with some crusty bread on the side.

The Chicken version of Pepe soup is said to clear the common cold!

Pepe Soup - Cows Foot

Another variation of the classic pepe soup uses cow's foot. The gelatine in the foot makes soup a little thicker and stickier. This makes the soup ideal to be eaten with some fresh bread, or with boiled cassava chunks.

3 Hours   Moderate

Ingredients:

- 2 cows feet (about 40cm each)
- 3 litres of water
- 3 onions, finely chopped
- 3 cloves of garlic
- 3 tomatoes, finely chopped
- 3 tablespoons of tomato concentrate paste
- 4 potatoes, peeled
- 2 kani chillies, finely chopped
- 1 kani chilli, whole
- 2 teaspoons of black pepper
- 2 bay leaves
- 50 millilitres of white vinegar
- 1 large Maggi cube
- 1 sweet pepper, seeds removed and finely chopped
- Salt & Pepper to taste

Method:

1. Clean the cows feet - if the skin hasn't been removed, remove it.
2. Cut the feet into pieces about 10cm each, and rinse off any excess bone shards under running water.
3. Bring the 3 litres of water to a boil, then add the pieces of cows foot.
4. Boil for an hour.
5. Add all the remaining ingredients except the potatoes.
6. Simmer for 40 minutes.
7. Add the potatoes, cut into large chunks - then simmer until the potatoes are cooked.
8. Check salt level and add salt if necessary.

The little meat on the cows foot should be falling off the bone by the time this is cooked. If you need to save time, use a pressure cooker and just add all the ingredients bar the potatoes and whole kani chilli at once. Then, simmer for 30 minutes with the potatoes and whole kani to cook those too.

Pepe Soup - Fish

A variation on the traditional pepper soup, the fish variety uses fish heads instead of the tail of the fish. This makes it a very cheap dish to make, and one of the most tasty versions of this fiery soup!

2 Hours   Moderate

Ingredients:

- 1kilograms of fish heads
- 3 large onions, finely chopped
- 3 tomatoes, finely chopped
- ½ cup palm oil
- 3 tablespoons tomato concentrate paste
- 3 kani chillies, finely chopped
- juice from 3-5 limes
- 1 large Maggi cube
- 3 bay leaves
- 1 litre of water
- ½ a cabbage, cut into 4
- 1 medium aubergine, cut into 8
- 1 sweet pepper, seeds removed and finely chopped
- Salt & Pepper to taste

Method:

1. Clean the fish heads by removing any scales and gills under running water.
2. Cut the fish heads lengthwise, to create 2 mirror halves from each head.
3. Marinate the fish heads in a mix of 1 teaspoon of salt, 1 teaspoon of black pepper and the lime juice for a few hours in the fridge.
4. Heat the oil and fry the onions until golden brown.
5. Add the tomatoes, tomato paste, kani chillies, and sweet pepper - fry for 5 minutes, stirring constantly.
6. Add the fish heads, with the marinade, and fry for 5 minutes.
7. Add all the other ingredients (water, Maggi cube, bay leaves, cabbage, and aubergine).
8. Simmer for 30 minutes, or until the broth has thickened to the consistency of a good soup.
9. Serve with white rice or Fufu.

If you want a less spicy soup, but still want the flavour of the kani chillies, remove the seeds from the chillies before cooking.

Pepe Soup - Oxtail

Pepe Soup, as the title suggests, is a pepper-based soup. As a kid growing up, I couldn't go near this fiery dish; but my mother went crazy for it. Try to avoid normal scotch bonnet chillies for this one, you really need the classic kani!

2.5 Hours   Moderate

Ingredients:

- 250 grams of tomato concentrate paste
- 700grams of oxtail, cut into disks
- 50milliliters of white vinegar
- 3 cloves of garlic, crushed
- 2 onions, finely chopped
- 5 tomatoes, finely chopped
- 2 tablespoons of kani chilli, finely chopped
- 2 whole kani chillies
- 1 litre of water
- 2 large Maggi cubes
- 3 potatoes, cut into cubes
- 3 carrots, cut into thirds
- 2 bay leaves
- tablespoon black pepper, finely ground
- 2 tablespoons of peanut oil

Method:

1. Marinade the oxtail in 1 teaspoon salt, 1 tablespoon black pepper, and vinegar for 4 hours in the fridge.
2. Heat the oil in a deep pan, then fry the onions until golden brown.
3. Add the garlic and oxtail, and fry for 2 minutes.
4. Add all the other ingredients and bring to a boil.
5. Simmer for 2 hours, with the lid on.
6. Serve with rice of Fufu.

For a quicker cooking time, make this in a pressure cooker - reduce the water by half and cook for 20 minutes under pressure.

Rice

Rice forms one of the staples for West African cooking. Eaten with most dishes, this is the base as meat and fish tend to be expensive.

40 Minutes   Moderate

Ingredients:

- 500g of rice
- Water

Method:

1. Clean the rice, by placing in a bowl and adding water, you will notice that the water becomes cloudy, this is the starch from the rice, drain the water and add fresh water again. Continue this until the water stays relatively clear (usually 3-4 times).
2. Drain the rice and place in a saucepan, add enough water so that water level is roughly 2cm above the rice. Place on the cooker and bring to the boil. Once boiling reduce heat, cover and continue to simmer for 20 minutes, the water should have been absorbed in this period of time.
3. Place the rice in a colander to remove any excess water. Transfer to a large serving bowl and enjoy.

For added authenticity, use "broken" rice - i.e. rice where each grain isn't intact.

Shackpa Plasas Stew

A very interesting stew, made in part with flowers. This can be easily made vegetarian by removing the beef and fish - the stew still tastes spectacular!

2 Hours   Moderate

Ingredients:

- 500 grams of hibiscus flower buds, thoroughly washed
- 1kilograms of beef
- 2 smoked bongas, washed and bones removed
- 2 sweet peppers, seeds removed
- 300 grams of peanuts, crushed
- 2 large Maggi cubes
- 4 onions, peeled
- 1 cup palm oil
- 2 kani chillies
- Salt & Pepper to taste

Method:

1. In a blender, mix the sweet peppers, onions and 1 kani chilli.
2. Heat the palm oil, then fry the beef.
3. Add the rest of the ingredients and 2 litres of water, except the flower buds.
4. Bring to a boil, then simmer for 1.5 hours or until the stew thickens.
5. Add the hibiscus flower buds and simmer for a further 30 minutes.

6. Serve over white rice.

For a visually stunning dish, keep a few uncooked flower buds aside. When serving, sprinkle a few uncooked flower blossoms over the top.

Sosfarin

Sosfarin is one of the cheaper Gambian dishes - and both the name and recipe show this. Sos-farin, or Sauce Farine (Flour Sauce in French) is essentially a spicy bechamel sauce, adapted over the years to the local ingredients and flavours.

1 Hour   Moderate

Ingredients:

- 1 litre of water
- 200 g flour
- 1 large Maggi cube
- 500 millilitres peanut or palm oil
- 3 tablespoons tomato concentrate
- 2 kani chillies
- 1 bay leaf
- 1 tablespoon lime juice
- 2 cloves of garlic, peeled
- 2 onions, peeled and coarsely chopped
- 7 tomatoes, coarsely chopped
- 1 teaspoon black peppercorns
- Salt & Pepper to taste

Method:

1. Blend the tomatoes, Maggi, tomato paste, garlic, black peppercorns and onions until a smooth paste is obtained.
2. Heat the oil in a deep, non-stick pan.

3. Once hot, add the paste and stir on high heat for 1-2 minutes, making sure the paste does not stick to the pan and burn.
4. Mix in the lime juice, chopped kani, the bay leaf and the water; then bring to a boil.
5. Allow to simmer for 20 minutes.
6. Mix in the flour, a little at a time, making sure no lumps are formed.
7. Mix well, and simmer for 10 minutes. The sauce will thicken during this time, so make sure you stir constantly to avoid it sticking to the pan.
8. Serve hot, over plain white rice.

If you're having trouble getting the flour to blend in smoothly, mix the flour with some water in the blender, then mix the smooth paste in with the soup. If you don't want this too spicy, instead of adding both kani chillies chopped, leave them whole - the resulting soup will be less spicy.

Supakanja

Supakanja is another of The Gambia's most famous dishes. This slightly slimy stew which incorporates fish and beef was a staple on Saturday evenings in our house (along with any leftover Domoda). Strongly recommended with an ice cold coke!

2-3 Hours   Simple

Ingredients:

- ½ kilograms of Okra (lady fingers) cut into small pieces
- 2 magi cubes
- 1-2 medium onions sliced
- 1 Bonga fish deboned and cleaned (smoked fish)
- 1 fish (snapper or lady fish) boiled, then flaked and deboned
- 200g stewing beef
- ½ kilograms of spinach or sorrel
- 2-3 magi cubes
- ½ cup of palm oil or peanut oil
- 1 to 2 kani whole
- 7 cups of water
- Salt & Red pepper to taste

Method:

1. In a large pot add ½ the oil and brown off the beef, once browned add onions and cook until the onions begin to brown a little.
2. Add all remaining ingredients and simmer for 1 to 2 hours or until the mixture begins to thicken. Add

remaining oil to the pot and stir. Continue to cook on a low heat until the oil comes up to the surface and you are ready to serve.

3. Serve on boiled rice.

Sweets

Sweets form a fantastic complement to any
Gambian feast. After the spicy kani, an array of
palate soothing sweets comes into play. Even
better, at a party or feast, the selection of sweets is
enough to make an adult drool - let alone a child!

Banana Cake

The Fajara Club used to be **the** place to be after school. They had cracked concrete tennis courts, a pool without too many algae and most importantly, an amazing banana cake! The original recipe had walnuts or peanuts inside - but as I'm not a fan of either of these in my banana cake, these have been omitted. You can always re-add them if you wish!

1.5 Hours   Simple

Ingredients:

- 125grams unsalted butter, at room temperature
- 1 cup sugar
- 2 eggs
- 2 cups flour
- 4 very ripe medium-small bananas
- ½ cup plain yoghurt
- ½ teaspoon baking powder
- 1 teaspoon baking soda

Method:

1. Preheat oven to 180°C.
2. Beat the eggs in a bowl, then add the butter and sugar and mix well.
3. Gradually add the flour, and keep mixing until uniform.
4. In a separate bowl, mash the bananas and mix with the yoghurt.
5. Mix the banana mix with the flour mix.

6. Bake in a loaf pan for 45-55 minutes - test if it is cooked by pricking with a toothpick. It should come out clean. As the cake rises and starts to set, lower the temperature to 140°C.

7. Sprinkle with icing sugar when serving; alternatively, put some slices of banana on the side while serving.

Baobab Sauce

The Baobab tree is one of the most vivid memories I have of The Gambia. It's commonly referred to as the upside down tree due to its looks, or the tree of life due to the fact that every piece from the root up serves a purpose.

25 Minutes   Simple

Ingredients:

- 2 cups of baobab fruit pulp with seeds (about 50 grams of seedless pulp)
- 1 cup groundnut paste or smooth peanut butter
- 500milliliters of water
- Sugar to taste

Method:

1. Bring the water to a boil, then remove from the heat.
2. Add the baobab fruit pulp and groundnut paste, and allow to simmer for a few minutes.
3. Agitate the mix, separating the pulp from the seeds.
4. Remove the seeds from the sauce.
5. Add sugar to taste.
6. Serve warm or cold, with porridge, Churah or Ruy.

If using pulp that has already been separated from the seeds, skip steps 3 and 4. For a western twist, try this with pancakes!

Bread and Coconut pudding

A Gambian variation of the popular bread pudding, this was a favourite of mine growing up. Mom would make it with and without the coconut, and it is absolutely stunning with a little custard!

1 Hour   Simple

Ingredients:

- ½ loaf or 1 baguette dry bread
- 250 millilitres milk
- 50 grams sugar
- 50 grams grated coconut
- 50 grams butter
- 3 eggs, beaten
- ¼ cup raisins
- ½ teaspoon vanilla flavouring

Method:

1. Pre-heat the oven to 160°C
2. Mix the milk with the sugar, and mix until all the sugar is dissolved. Then add the vanilla flavouring and the eggs. Mix well.
3. Cut the bread into strips about 2cm wide. Spread the butter on the bread fingers, until all the butter is used up. Sprinkle the coconut into the bread, so that it sticks to the butter.
4. In a loaf baking tin, put the bread in a thatched/criss-cross pattern. Sprinkle a few raisins here and there.

5. Pour the milk mixture over the bread and allow to sit for 15 minutes to allow the bread to go soggy.

6. Bake for 40 minutes - then allow to cool before serving.

This pudding is a great way to get rid of any leftover bread!

Chakery

A splendid desert made using couscous which is then covered with dairy based sauce.

30 Minutes   Simple

Ingredients:

- Couscous
- 500milliliters plain yogurt
- 250milliliters unsweetened evaporated milk
- 250milliliters sour cream
- 1 can of pineapple chopped
- Sugar to taste
- Vanilla extract (for flavouring only, 1 teaspoon)

Method:

1. In a saucepan combine all the ingredients except for the Couscous, and heat gently until the sugar has dissolved and all ingredients are incorporated.
2. While the sauce is cooking prepare the couscous, following the instructions on the packaging.
3. Once the couscous is ready, serve in bowls and ladle the sauce over the top.

Instead of using plain yogurt and unsweetened evaporated milk, you can substitute them for the following, Vanilla yogurt and regular evaporated milk, by doing so you can avoid adding additional sugar or other fruits.

Churahgerteh

Chura Gerte is a typical breakfast porridge made with rice and peanuts. Very easy to make, filling and extremely tasty!

1.5 Hours   Simple

Ingredients:

- 2 litres of water
- 500 grams rice
- 500 grams peanuts
- concentrated milk
- salt & sugar to taste

Method:

1. Pound the peanuts in a mortar & pestle until smooth.
2. Add the rice and peanut powder to the water.
3. Bring to a boil, then add ½ teaspoon of salt.
4. Boil for 10 minutes, stirring constantly.
5. Lower the heat and cook for 60 minutes - the rice will be overcooked and the consistency should be similar to porridge.
6. Serve warm with concentrated milk and sugar to taste on the side.

The milk and sugar are optional, but if you want to try something healthier, try replacing the sugar with honey, maple syrup or agave syrup! Alternatively add some papaya jam or baobab pulp!

Jack Fruit Tart

The jack fruit is a massive fruit that grows mainly in Asia. That said, a few trees are scattered around The Gambia - including one behind the football pitch in the old BAES campus in Bakau - but that's a different story. The fruit looks a lot like the Durian, but luckily, doesn't smell as bad.

1 Hour   Simple

Ingredients:

- 1 pack of frozen short-crust pastry
- ½ cup of butter
- 1 cup or fresh, very ripe, jackfruit - seeds removed
- 2 eggs
- ¼ cup condensed milk, sweetened
- 50g cream cheese (Philadelphia or vache qui rit)
- ½ teaspoon vanilla extract
- 1 tablespoon plain white flour

Method:

1. Preheat the oven to 180C..
2. Butter a pie-pan or cake-pan, then put in the fridge until the pan is cold (set the remaining butter aside).
3. Defrost the pastry, and press into the pan, forming a crust 1cm thick - return to the fridge to keep it cool.
4. Mix all the other ingredients in a blender, including the remaining butter - blend until a smooth mix is obtained.

5. Pour the mix into the base, then bake for 30-40 minutes. To check if it's cooked, insert a toothpick into the middle - it should come out clean.
6. Allow to cool before serving - ideally with some vanilla ice cream or baobab sauce!

Lah with Gini Jobe

Lah (or Lak) is a millet porridge, served with Gini Jobe (Boabab sauce). A typical desert in Gambia, it is a truly spectacular end to a feast which sooths even the most pungent of kani!

5 Hours   Complex

Ingredients:

- 2 cups of millet flour
- 1 litre water
- 1 cup of baobab fruit
- 1 cup of smooth peanut butter
- ½ teaspoon nutmeg
- 1 teaspoon vanilla essence
- 1 tablespoon butter (optional)
- 1 tablespoon sugar (to taste)

Method:

1. Mix the millet flour with water to form a dough.
2. Split the dough into balls, about 5 centimetres in diameter. Set aside.
3. Soak the baobab fruit in clean water for 4 hours
4. Agitate to remove the seeds and fibre.
5. Add the peanut butter to the baobab water, then mix until smooth.
6. Add the vanilla and nutmeg, mix well and refrigerate
7. Bring 1 litre of water to a boil.
8. Add the millet balls and dissolve.

9. Simmer for 10 minutes, or until the consistency of porridge.
10. Allow to cool (optional, stir in butter).
11. To serve mix the millet porridge, the Boabab sauce and sugar to taste.

Naanburu

Naanburu is a favourite desert - with more variations in the recipe than families in The Gambia. The recipe below is my version, which is a variation on the classic. It removes the larger chunks and leaves a smoother pudding like mix.

30 Minutes   Simple

Ingredients:

- 2 litres milk
- 100 grams pounded rice, or coarse rice flour
- 3 cups of baobab fruits
- 200g sugar

Method:

1. Mix 1 litre of milk with the baobab in a non-stick pan and bring to a gentle boil.
2. Agitate with a potato masher, until all the pulp has detached from the Boabab seeds. Strain the mix, removing the seeds and fibre.
3. Add the sugar to the strained mix, and put on the fire on very low heat.
4. Mix the remaining cold milk with the pounded rice, until no lumps remain.
5. Stirring constantly, add the cold milk to the milk in the pan. Once the two are completely mixed, raise the heat a little and simmer for 5-10 minutes, or until a porridge-like consistency is obtained.
6. Allow to cool in the fridge before serving.

Papaya jam

Papaya jam is the ultimate snack when put on bread and butter; but it holds its par served with porridge; and can even be poured onto jack fruit tarts to add some sweetness. Ideally you should use the tiny "Chinese" papayas sold at Bakau market, but any other papaya will do - even green ones!

5 Hours   Simple

Ingredients:

- 1kilograms of papaya flesh (no seeds, no skin)
- 500grams of sugar
- 1 lime

Method:

1. Chop the papaya into small cubes and put into a large pan.
2. Add the sugar, and the juice from the lime and stir well.
3. Allow to sit in the fridge for 3-4 hours - the papaya will go very soft, and the juices will come out.
4. Bring the mixture to a boil on medium heat, then simmer for 40 minutes, stirring constantly.
5. Allow to cool before serving!

If jarring this, boil the jars and lids for 1 hour to sterilize them. Then, pour & seal the jars while the mixture is still hot. This will create a vacuum which will preserve the jam for about a year.

Rice pudding

Rice puddings do not need any description, it is a classic dish around the world. The following recipe has a Gambian twist to it and uses coconut milk and evaporated milk.

1.5 Hours   Simple

Ingredients:

- 250gm White Rice
- 500milliliters coconut milk
- 500milliliters evaporated milk
- ¼ cup sugar (you can add more to taste)
- 50gm butter

Method:

1. Clean the rice under cold running water to wash away the starch, when the water runs clear set aside until ready to use.
2. In a pan combine the coconut milk, evaporated milk sugar and rice. Place on the cooker and bring to the boil. Once the milk begins to boil, add the butter and then reduce the temperature and continue to simmer for 30 minutes.
3. After the first 30 minutes remove the lid and begin stirring the rice. Keep cooking as stirring frequently for a further 30 to 40 minutes or until you get the desired, soft creamy consistency.
4. Once ready ladle into bowls and serve.

If using pudding rice cooking time may vary, bear this in mind when as pudding rice tends to take longer to cook than white rice.

For added flavour you can add ground cinnamon, nutmeg, mango or other soft sweet fruits to the milk and sugar mixture.

Ruy

Cous Cous in Gambia is not what westerners are normally used to; Cous Cous (or simply Cous) is Millet, a small seeded type of grain. Ruy, or more commonly Cous Cous Porridge, is another typical breakfast - more commonly eaten in the rural villages where cous is grown for local consumption.

45 Minutes   Simple

Ingredients:

- 500 grams millet flour
- 3 litres water
- 1 teaspoon salt
- 4 tablespoons sugar

Method:

1. Mix the flour with a little water and knead until a dough is formed - this prevents lumps.
2. Bring the rest of the water to a boil, then gradually add the cous dough in small pieces, stirring constantly.
3. Once all the dough has been added, boil for 3 minutes on high heat, stirring constantly.
4. Reduce the heat and simmer for 30 minutes on low heat, the porridge will go clear.
5. Allow to cool, then serve with sugar.

If you cannot find Millet flour, blend some millet grain in a food processor until it has the consistency of flour. Instead of sugar, try with honey, jam, peanut butter or concentrated milk

Drinks

Drinks play an important role The Gambia. Not only does the liquid content serve an important role in rehydrating people, but they also tempt the palate!

Attaya

Attaya is more than just a green tea. Attaya is a way of life. Brewing a pot of attaya starts with a Chinese green tea called "gunpowder" - named thus after it's leaves which are balled up to protect them in transport. The preparation can take up to an hour, where the tea is poured from increasing heights into shot-glass sized glasses. When finally served, it is scalding hot and extremely strong - the polite way to drink it is to slurp it, skimming off the top with some air.

The recipe below is slightly simplified.

30 Minutes   Simple

Ingredients:

- 25milliliters of dry "gunpowder" green tea
- 200milliliters of water
- 25milliliters of sugar

Method:

1. Bring the water to a boil in a pan with a lid (ideally with a spout).
2. Add the tea leaves and sugar, cover and boil for 5 minutes.
3. Pour one glass-worth out into a glass.
4. Transfuse the contents of the glass into 3 different glasses, one at a time, thus warming up all 5 glasses.
5. Pour back into the pan.
6. Boil for 5 minutes.

7. Repeat steps 3-6 a further 6 times (for a total of 7 "pours") - each time the tea is poured, the height from which it is poured must increase. This takes some practice, but serves a purpose - it creates a frothy head on the tea.
8. The tea content should boil down to about 120milliliters - pour out into 4 small, clear glasses; ensuring that it is poured from sufficient height to create a foamy head
9. Serve the eldest person first!

Ideally served under a mango tree while chatting to friends.

BAES Brew

BAES Brew, or the Witches' Healthy Brew, is a concoction that we came up with as a class assignment for Halloween in BAES, the American School in Gambia. At the time, the school was across the street from the Bakau Army barracks - some of my fondest memories remain on those grounds.

5 Minutes   Simple

Ingredients:

- 2 cans of Perrier (4x 330ml)
- 2 cups of freshly squeezed orange juice
- 100cl of freshly squeezed lime juice
- 2 tablespoons of plastic bugs
- 4 glasses of ice cubes
- A few drops of green food colouring

Method:

1. Gently mix the juices and the water together.
2. Fill four glasses with ice cubes.
3. Pour the juice & water over the ice and sprinkle a few bugs in each glass.
4. Put 2 drops of food colouring in each glass, do not mix!
5. Serve immediately.

Bwi

Bwi or Bouyeh is a drink made of the Baobab fruit. As a child, we would scrape the hairy coating off the large green pods - this "fur" makes for a fantastic prank. If applied to your victims skin, it would cause an intense itching! Inside the hard shell of the fruit, there are lots of little black seeds coated in edible white pods.

5 Hours   Simple

Ingredients:

- 2 cups of baobab fruit pulp with seeds (about 30 grams of seedless pulp)
- 1 litre of water
- 1 tablespoon sugar (more to taste)

Method:

1. Bring the water to a boil, then remove from the heat.
2. Add the baobab fruit pulp and allow to sit for 4 hours, the pulp will hydrate and detach from the seeds.
3. Agitate the mix, further separating the pulp from the seeds - the water should be an opaque off-white colour.
4. Remove the seeds and fibrous material from the drink.
5. Strain with a clean cloth and add sugar to taste - the drink needs to be very sweet.
6. Chill and serve over ice!

For a more velvety taste, add a cup of pineapple juice and ½ a teaspoon of vanilla extract.

Daharr (Tamarind Juice)

Every year there would be a food fair organized by the Women's Organization in Abuko Village. My mother's friend Awa would make juices, Daharr, Bwi, Ginger Ale, and Wonjo. Below is one of the simpler recipes for Daharr - or tamarind juice. While an acquired taste, the drink is extremely refreshing and can quench anyone's thirst with barely a glassful!

20 Minutes   Simple

Ingredients:

- 2 cups fresh peeled tamarind pods or ½ cup tamarind pulp
- Juice from 4 limes
- 2 litres water
- Sugar to taste
- Ice

Method:

1. Bring the water to a boil and add the tamarind.
2. Agitate with a potato masher (or similar) until the pulp has detached from the seeds.
3. Simmer for 10 minutes.
4. Allow to cool, then strain.
5. Add the lime juice and sugar to taste.
6. Serve chilled over ice!

Adjust the lime juice and sugar to make a slightly more tangy drink. Traditionally, the drink is served extremely sweet.

Ginger Beer

A sweet and spicy drink with variations around the world.

20 Minutes   Simple

Ingredients:

- 250g ginger
- 2 cups sugar
- 3 litres of water

Method:

1. Peel the ginger roots. (use a teaspoon to scrape the skin of the ginger, this method is easy and doesn't waste the ginger).
2. Using a fine grater or blender/chopper, grate/blitz the ginger until it is a paste.
3. In a large jug combine the ginger, sugar and water and mix until the sugar has dissolved, taste, you can add more sugar, water or ginger to suit your taste.
4. Place in the fridge to chill.
5. Before serving the ginger beer you may want to strain it to remove any of the ginger fibres.
6. Serve in a glass with lots of ice.

As a personal preference I like to put all the ingredients in a large pot and bring to the boil.

Once boiling remove from heat and let cool naturally, after it has cooled you can strain the ginger juice, and transfer to a jug or bottle to chill in the fridge.

I find that by heating up the mixture and letting it steep you get more flavour from the ginger, it also ensure that the sugar is dissolved completely, you can also adjust the quantities of all ingredients to suit your taste.

I also like to add the juice of ½ a lime to the glass before serving.

Guava Juice

One of my friends had a large guava tree in front of his house - in addition to marvelling at its most curious bark and climbing up its limbs, we would spend entire afternoons trying to reach those most elusive of fruits - the ripe guava. Sadly, the birds would reach them before us; but when we did get them, it was guava juice time!

20 Minutes   Simple

Ingredients:

- 4 large ripe guavas
- 2 litres of water
- 1 lime
- Sugar to taste

Method:

1. Bring the water to a boil.
2. Peel the guavas and chop the inner pulp.
3. Add the pulp from the guavas and simmer for 10 minutes while agitating with a potato masher.
4. Allow the mix to cool.
5. Add the juice from the lime (optional) and sugar to taste.
6. Strain thoroughly, using the back of a spoon to pass the pulp through the sieve.
7. Chill and enjoy over ice!

Lime Juice

Given the sugar and water content, this probably wouldn't make the classification of juice - but my grandmother wasn't someone you argued with! We had a lime tree next to the kitchen, and every day "mama" (my grandmother) and "Binta" (the maid) would make lime juice. Nothing more refreshing!

15 Minutes   Simple

Ingredients:

- 1kilograms fresh limes
- 250 grams sugar
- 4 glasses of ice
- water to taste

Method:

1. Squeeze the limes into a jug.
2. Add sugar in a ratio of 1:2 to lime juice (50grams of sugar for 100milliliters of lime juice).
3. Pour over the ice, then add water - for a weak blend 1 part of lime/sugar to 10 parts water works quite well.

You can freeze the lime/sugar mix in an ice cube tray. Then, just pop the ice-cubes into the water when you want a drink!

Papu's Banana Smoothie

Papu was a little kid who grew up in The Gambia - and let me tell you, he was a right pain! He was commonly referred to as "Sai Sai" (naughty, pest) but boy did he have a taste for good food!

The simple recipe below is his special banana smoothie - this has been my secret since I was a kid, so use it with care! It's thirst quenching, full of good fruit stuff and calcium.

5 Minutes   Simple

Ingredients:

- 4 bananas, ripe
- 2 glasses of milk
- 1 glass of ice
- 1 lime
- 8 mint leaves, washed

Method:

1. Peel the bananas, and quickly cut into large disks.
2. Put the cut bananas, milk and half the ice in a blender.
3. Blend until smooth (2-3 minutes).
4. Add the juice of a lime.
5. Put the remaining ice into 4 glasses with 2 mint leaves in each glass.
6. Pour and enjoy immediately!

Thé, de la Vie

Mauritanian tea, for lack of a better name is the tea cooked by the corner shops, commonly referred to as Mauritanian boutiques. A large number of Mauritanian's came to Gambia during the Ould Daddah era (1960-1978) when the president brought Mauritania into conflict with Algeria and Morocco over the Western Saharan strip. With the refugees arrived new palates, ingredients and recipes!

The tea below is also prepared in parts of Morocco, Senegal and parts of Gambia. The leaves are traditionally re-brewed 3 times and accompanied with the proverb: "The first glass is as bitter as life, the second glass is as strong as love while the third glass is as gentle as death".

45 Minutes   Simple

Ingredients:

- ❦ 50 grams of loose "gunpowder" green tea
- ❦ 30 grams of fresh mint leaves
- ❦ 20 grams of fresh sage leaves
- ❦ 60 grams of sugar
- ❦ 1500milliliters of water

Method:

1. Bring 500milliliters water to a boil, then add the tea leaves.
2. Boil for 2 minutes, then add the rest of the leaves and 20 grams of sugar.

3. Boil for 5, or until the leaves go soft and the tea has a pungent aroma of mint and sage.
4. Serve first round, or the round of life.
5. Add a further 500milliliters of water and 20 grams of sugar to the leaves and boil for 10 minutes.
6. Serve the second round, or the round as sweet love.
7. Add the final 500milliliters of water and the final 20grams of sugar and boil for 10 minutes.
8. Serve the final round, or the round as gentle death.

I must confess that the precise recipe was taught to me by a toothless, elderly, alchemist near Tizi-n-Test, Morocco during the Timbuktu Rally - but that's a different story. That said, it's very similar to the one made by Saidou, who ran the corner shop near my compound in Cape Point.

Wonjo

Wonjo, also known as soup juice or "bissap" is an infusion based on the "Hibiscus sabdariffa" flower, more commonly known as Roselle. While the entire plant can be eaten and used in various recipes, Wonjo makes use of the red flowers' fleshy petals.

As any very popular recipe, there are a plethora of variations. The version below was taught to me by Binta, and I while my Wonjo will never equal the one she made, it's a delectable drink none-the-less.

15 Minutes   Simple

Ingredients:

- 2 cups dry Wonjo flowers
- 1-2 cups sugar
- A sprig of mint
- ½ tsp of vanilla extract
- 2 cups pineapple juice
- ¼ cup freshly squeezed lime juice
- 2 litres of drinking water
- 4 glasses of ice cubes

Method:

1. Rinse the Wonjo flowers , discard the water. Do not soak the dry flowers.
2. Bring the 2 litres of water to a boil.
3. As soon as the water starts boiling, add the flowers and remove from heat.
4. Allow to steep for 10-15 minutes.

5. Strain the liquid, discard the flowers.
6. Add the pineapple juice, lime juice, mint leaves, vanilla extract; mix well and allow to cool.
7. Add sugar to taste, then chill for several hours in the refrigerator.
8. Serve over ice.

For a different flavour, try adjusting the levels of sugar and lime juice. Alternatively, mix with sparkling water for a fizzy drink.

Toubab Dishes

Toubab, an endearing word used to refer to Caucasians, quite literally means "two bobs". A bob was a slang term for a shilling, and it has been suggested that two shillings was the price that was shouted to foreign slave-traders as they made their way through villages. Others have suggested that two shillings was the salary paid to workers. Whatever the etymology of the term "toubab", it's one that has become an integral part of Gambian culture - as have the "toubabs".

Along with other influences, the toubabs have brought to Gambia a selection of dishes which quickly became classics in the authors' view (and on their taste-buds!). Thus, while the traditional Gambian meal doesn't include starters as such - the following fusion dishes are only found in Gambia and are as intricate a part of the culinary culture as the toubabs are in everyday life.

Calypso Prawn Cocktail

The Calypso Prawn Cocktail is named in honour of a beach bar in Cape Point. In the early 90's I learnt how to bill things to my mother's tab - before I could write my name! (for those curious, I would write "PND" on the bill, which stood for "Papu, Nadia, and Dayal" - or my nickname and my parent's names). Large part of the tab was of Prawn Cocktails - needless to say, I've preserved this recipe and adapted it over the years!

30 Minutes   Simple

Ingredients:

- 1kilograms Raw Shell-On Prawns (if using peeled prawns, use 500gr)
- ½ cup Ketchup
- ½ cup Mayonnaise
- 1 Medium Grapefruit

To Serve:

- 1 lime, cut into 4 wedges
- 8-12 Salad Leaves
- A Sprinkle of Paprika

Method:

1. If raw, boil the prawns until they turn an pinky-orange colour.
2. Allow to cool, then peel the prawns, removing the head and tail.

3. While the prawns cool, peel the grapefruit. Split into segments, and then remove the skin around the segments.

4. Mix the ketchup and mayonnaise together and whisk with a fork until a smooth and uniform pink sauce is attained.

5. Gently fold the prawns and grapefruit into the pink sauce.

6. To serve, put the mix onto a bed of 2-3 salad leaves, or in a cup over the salad leaves. Sprinkle with paprika and add a wedge of lime.

Try this recipe with shrimps, crayfish, of lobster for a different flavour. Alternatively, substitute the salad for rocket leaves for an extra kick.

Fish in Foil

This is a childhood favourite of mine. I remember every Sunday going to the beach and being serve freshly caught fish grilled with potatoes and onions and spices. A perfect dish for a warm summers day spent with friends and family.

60 Minutes   Simple

Ingredients:

- 1 medium whole red snapper, if not available sea-bass will be a great substitute (scaled and gutted)
- 1 onion sliced
- 1 kani chilli
- 1-2 cloves of garlic, peeled
- 1 medium to large potato chipped
- 1 tablespoon parsley, chopped
- 1 teaspoon dry thyme
- 1 Lemon
- 2 tablespoon vegetable oil
- Salt and black pepper

Method:

1. Cut slashes into the fish about 4 per side, they should be deep enough to pierce the skin but not reach the bone.
2. Combine the juice of 1 lemon, crushed garlic, sliced kani chilli, parsley, thyme, salt, black pepper and approximately 2 tablespoons of oil. Once combined rub into the fish.

3. Layer the onions and potatoes in the middle of the foil and season with salt, black pepper and oil. Then place the marinated fish on top of the onions and potatoes and drizzle with the remaining marinade.
4. Close the foil and place on the grill for approximately 40 minutes.

The dish can be made in the oven (180 degrees Celsius) for about 30 minutes or until the fish is cooked, cooking time may vary, depending on the size of the fish or the cooking method.

Fish Soup a La Valbonne

La Valbonne was Valeria's complex - Gambia's only luxurious casino, the fanciest restaurant (and in the later years, a slot machine room, a night club and a cocktail bar). I still remember Valeria with fondness. She was the friendliest 2-meter tall lady the planet has ever seen - though if she didn't like you it would be deadly clear; and usually followed by a string of insults.

Anyhow - my mother used to make a stunning fish soup in Gambia, mixing ladyfish, snapper, sole, shrimps, lobsters, crabs and more. The only other place that had a similar dish was at La Valbonne. This recipe is my mother's original, which is named in honour of Valeria and her restaurant.

45 Minutes   Simple

Ingredients:

- 800 grams of mixed fish (ladyfish, red snapper, sole fish, shrimps, small lobsters, crab claws, etc)
- 500grams tinned tomatoes
- 1 handful of fresh basil
- 1 teaspoon of oregano
- 5 cloves of garlic, peeled and thinly sliced
- 1 tablespoon of olive oil
- ½ teaspoon of salt
- 1 large onion, finely chopped
- 2 teaspoons of parsley
- 4 thick slices of crusty bread (Tapalapa or ciabatta)

Method:

1. Heat the oil in a large pan.
2. Add the onions and garlic allowing them to brown.
3. Once golden brown, add the tomatoes, the parsley and the basil.
4. Allow to simmer for 20 minutes on medium heat.
5. Add the fish, diced in large cubes.
6. Allow to simmer until all the fish is cooked.
7. In the meanwhile, toast the slices of bread.
8. To serve, put a slice of the crunchy bread on a bowl, then pour over the fish soup and sprinkle with oregano.

My mother would originally do this recipe using fish that still had the bones in. While this does add to the flavour of the stock, some guests may not be able to remove the bones. As such, some may prefer to use boned fish fillets.

Leybato's Pepper Steak

Leybato was a bar and restaurant in Fajara - it was <u>the</u> place to go for a pepper steak. For years when asked where I wanted to go eat lunch, the answer was Leybato. Years later, I came across a recipe that Leybato had released for their pepper steak - the adaptation below incredibly close to the original! The only things missing are the straw umbrellas, the beach and the sun!

40 Minutes   Simple

Ingredients:

- 4 pieces of tender beef fillet
- 4 tablespoons black peppercorns
- 1 large onion, finely chopped
- 1 large tomato, finely chopped
- 4 cloves of garlic, finely chopped
- 2 teaspoons paprika
- 200 grams of butter
- 2 tablespoons of flour
- 2 large Maggi cubes

Method:

1. Melt half the butter in a frying pan, then fry the fillets until medium rare.
2. Remove the fillet from the pan and wrap in aluminium foil to keep warm & moist.
3. Add the onion, tomato, garlic, paprika, rest of the butter, and Maggi cubes to the pan.
4. Simmer until the onions are soft.

5. Add 2 tablespoons of flour, and stir until smooth - the flour will thicken the sauce.

6. Serve warm with fries, preferably with the view of a sunny beach!

If you like your meat burnt, you can obviously make this recipe cooking the steak "well done" instead of rare.

Lobster with Tomato and Onion Pepper Sauce

The description is in the title ☺

60 Minutes   Simple

Ingredients:

- Akra dipping sauce without vermicelli
- 2 fresh lobsters

Method:

1. Cut the lobsters in half and clean, you can ask your fishmonger to do this for you.
2. Once the lobsters are cut and cleaned, ladle the sauce over the top of the flesh and making sure to cover it completely.
3. Heat a heavy skillet and place the Lobster shell side down on the skillet and cook for about 5 minutes, then transfer the skillet into a preheated oven (180 degrees Celsius) and cook for a further 30 minutes or until the lobster is cooked. Note that cooking times may vary depending on the size of the lobster and method of cooking.
4. Once cooked serve with a salad, rice or fries the possibilities are endless.

I personally prefer cooking the lobster on the BBQ, just place on the BBQ and cover. Cook until lobster is done.

Another alternative is:
1. Remove the lobster meat from the claws and shell, and cut it into 1 cm thick pieces.
2. Heat the shells in the oven until cooked through (they should be orange in colour).
3. In a pan heat up some oil and add the Akra dipping sauce, once it comes to the boil add the lobster and cook until the lobster is done.
4. Spoon the lobster into the shells and serve.

One could also use crab as an alternative to lobster in the above variation but instead of removing the crab from the shell, just break it up into bits (claws and so on) and cook in the sauce, this would be a similar cooking method to Thai black pepper crab.

Mom's pumpkin soup

Whenever she would find a nice, ripe pumpkin in Bakau market, mom would make (and still does) a pumpkin soup. This creamy dish is incredibly simple, and even more tasty! Perfect on those colder evenings, it's great with a some crusty bread!

45 Minutes Simple

Ingredients:

- 500 grams of peeled pumpkin flesh, cut into cubes
- 300milliliters milk
- 2 tablespoons thick cream
- 2 tablespoons butter
- Salt & pepper to taste

Method:

1. Put the pumpkin in a pan with a small amount of water (about half a glass). Simmer until the pumpkin is soft.
2. Add the butter; then gradually add the milk. Simmer for 20 minutes.
3. Before serving, add the cream and a pinch of salt. Dust with black pepper when serving.

For a more authentic taste, mom say's you should allow guests to add their own black pepper, olive oil and parmesan cheese at the table.

Nadia's Sipa Sipa

As much as I would like to claim the credits for inventing this recipe, it was passed to me by my mother would make the most delectable sipa-sipa (prawns/shrimp) ever!

I can still remember haggling for sipa-sipa at Bakau market, and always asking for an extra can of smaller ones to use as bait at the Old Cape Road bridge. Try to get raw shrimps to make this one!

30 Minutes   Simple

Ingredients:

- 500grams of raw shrimps
- 1 small tomato
- 1 small onion
- 1 teaspoon of parsley, finely chopped
- 3 tablespoons of white flour
- 1 lime
- 1 glass of white wine
- 2 teaspoons of oil
- Salt & Pepper

Method:

1. Heat the oil in a non-stick pan.
2. Remove the head and peel the raw shrimps.
3. Toss the peeled shrimps in the white flour, evenly (but lightly) coating them.

4. When hot, add the onion and tomato - cook at high heat for one minute stirring constantly.
5. Reduce the heat and add the juice from half of the lime and the shrimps.
6. When the shrimps start turning pinky-orange, add the juice from the other half of the lime, the white wine and a pinch of salt to taste.
7. Do not cover, cook on medium-high heat for 3-4 minutes or until the wine has been absorbed and turned into a rich gravy.

Although my mother's recipe, I do make some changes every now and then... My favourite is to replace the onion with some garlic and add a dash of Worchester sauce. Give it a try!

Pickled Kani

This one is a dead simple recipe I came up with after moving out of The Gambia. I found that getting the right chillies for Gambian cooking was very difficult as most scotch bonnets are all heat and no taste. So I started freezing kani chillies and bringing them back from Gambia - but even that didn't work too well. Finally, I found that pickling them works a treat! They retain all their flavour and can be used in just about any recipe.

30 Minutes   Simple

Ingredients:

- 2 litres of white vinegar
- 500 grams of fresh kani chillies, washed
- 2 litres of water
- 4 tablespoons salt
- Pickling jars (or old jam jars, thoroughly cleaned)

Method:

1. Bring the water to a boil, then add the salt and about 100milliliters of the vinegar to the water.
2. Adding the cold vinegar will cause the water to stop boiling, as soon as it boils again, throw in the kani chillies.
3. Leave the chillies in the water for no more than 5-10 seconds - this serves to disinfect them and kill any bacteria that would cause them to rot.
4. Quickly strain the chillies, and put into the jars.
5. Cover with the remaining vinegar and seal the jars.

6. Store in a cool, dry, and dark place until you're ready to use them!

As the vinegar is added cold, there is no vacuum created in the jars. As such, this relies on the antibacterial properties of the vinegar to stop the kani from rotting. If you want to store them for long periods; sterilize the jars in boiling water for 1-hour or so. Then bring the vinegar to a boil as well before adding to the chillies in the jars.

Roasted Water Chestnuts

Sarkis was the older brother of a common friend of ours, his cook (Mary) had a recipe for water chestnuts that was delectable!

The following is the recipe, as best as we can remember it, for these.

20 Minutes   Simple

Ingredients:

- ❧ 2 tins of water chestnuts
- ❧ 1 packet of streaky bacon, smoked
- ❧ 2 cloves of garlic, peeled and crushed
- ❧ 1 cup of ketchup
- ❧ 2 teaspoons of sugar

Method:

1. Preheat oven to 200°C.
2. In a blender, mix the ketchup, garlic and sugar.
3. Wrap the chestnuts in the bacon and bake until crispy (about 5-7 minutes).
4. Transfer the crispy bacon wrapped chestnuts to a service plats and pour the sauce liberally over them.
5. Serve piping hot!

Senegambia Grilled Prawns

The following was a recipe passed on by the executive chef of the Senegambia hotel at the time. A rich and luxurious dish of shrimps flambéed with cognac and served with chilli and lime sauce. Our thanks to Jonathan for teaching us the foundation of this recipe (and apologies for the adaptations we've made over the years).

30 Minutes   Moderate

Ingredients:

- 800grams raw peeled shrimps
- 60 grams of butter split into 3 equal portions
- 1 small glass of cognac
- 2 teaspoons of kani, finely chopped
- 1 tablespoon of lime juice
- 50milliliters of tomato ketchup
- 1 tablespoon of Worcestershire sauce
- 2 tablespoons of chopped garlic
- 2 tablespoons of chopped coriander

Method:

1. In a frying pan, melt 20grams of butter on medium heat.
2. Fry the shrimps in the pan, until pinky-orange, then raise the heat to maximum.
3. On high heat, add the glass of cognac (this will catch fire and flare up, so be careful!).
4. Remove the shrimps from the pan.

5. Add 20grams of butter to the juices still left in the pan, along with the lime juice, tomato ketchup, and Worcestershire sauce.
6. Simmer for 2 minutes.
7. Remove from the heat and add the shrimps and the last 20grams of butter.
8. Sprinkle with the coriander and serve immediately.

These are great with some Tapalapa sticks to mop up the sauce!

US Embassy Chilli

The following chilli was adapted from the original made by the U.S. Ambassador's Secretary and won the first prize for "best tasting" in the 1996 chilli cook-off in Banjul. My thanks with Joyce Wood for sharing this so many years ago!

2 Hours   Simple

Ingredients:

- 4 medium onions, peeled and coarsely chopped
- 3 cloves of garlic, peeled and crushed
- ¼ cup peanut oil
- 1 can of tinned tomatoes
- 3 cans of tinned red kidney beans
- 1 kani chilli, finely chopped
- 1kilograms of minced beef
- 1 teaspoon oregano
- 2 teaspoons salt
- 2 bay leaves
- ¼ cup chilli powder
- 3 tablespoons cider vinegar

Method:

1. Heat the oil and brown the onions until golden brown in a large non-stick pan.
2. Add the oregano, bay leaves, and beef - stir fry until the beef is cooked.

3. Add half the chilli powder, the kani chilli, tomatoes, 2 cans of kidney beans - simmer for 90 minutes on a very low flame.
4. Add the remaining ingredients, and simmer for a further 15 minutes stirring constantly.
5. Enjoy with plain white rice!

Valeria's Penne

Valeria was the owner of the "La Valbonne" restaurant; and she taught me how to make her secret "Penne, Pomodoro, Panna e Piselli" a recipe which has been a closely guarded secret of mine. I can claim that it is thanks solely to that recipe that my friend Jacob still frequents me!

4 Hours   Simple

Ingredients:

- 500 grams of "Penne" pasta
- 250milliliters of double cream
- 3 cans of tinned tomatoes
- 100 grams of peas
- 3 cloves of garlic, peeled and sliced finely
- 1 large onion, finely diced
- 1 glass of red wine (Barbera preferred)
- a handful of fresh basil leaves
- 1 carrot, peeled and finely chopped
- 1 stick of celery, finely chopped
- 5 tablespoons of olive oil
- 5 tablespoons of coarse sea salt
- 1 large Maggi cube
- Salt & Pepper to taste

Method:

    To make the sauce;

1. Heat 3 tablespoons of oil in a deep pan, then fry the onions until they are soft and golden

2. Add the garlic, carrot and celery and stir fry on medium heat for 2-3 minutes.
3. Raise the heat to the highest setting, and add the wine.
4. Stir for 1-2 minutes, then mix in the tomatoes and the Maggi cube.
5. Cover with a lid, and allow to simmer on a very low flame for 3 hours.

    To make the pasta:
6. Bring 5 litres of water to a boil, then add 5 tablespoons of salt.
7. Boil the pasta for 1 minutes LESS than the packet instructs.
8. Drain the pasta and put back into the pan, add the remaining 2 tablespoons of oil and stir.
9. Add the tomato sauce, peas, double cream and most of the basil leaves roughly chopped and stir.
10. When serving, put a whole basil leaf on each plate.

When boiling pasta, a common mistake is to put too little water. To prevent the pasta from sticking, you should use 1 litre of water and 1 tablespoon of salt for every 100 grams of dry pasta you intend to cook.

Thank you for reading this far. Unfortunately, the book has reached the end - though the experience does not end here! Grab your favourite recipe, your best friend and get cooking!

We would love to hear from you - if you have any comments, suggestions, ideas or generally want to chat about Gambian cooking, email:

authors@saharanpress.com

If you have a restaurant in The Gambia, and want a recipe you make featured in the next edition of this book, email:

editor@'saharanpress.com

Index

The Saharan Press

Part of the Eo Vita Group

ISBN 9781908797001

9 781908 797001